I0023412

Edward Beck

A Packet of Seeds Saved by an Old Gardner

Second Edition

Edward Beck

A Packet of Seeds Saved by an Old Gardner
Second Edition

ISBN/EAN: 9783337129149

Printed in Europe, USA, Canada, Australia, Japan

Cover: Foto ©Andreas Hilbeck / pixelio.de

More available books at **www.hansebooks.com**

A
PACKET OF SEEDS

SAVED BY

AN OLD GARDENER.

Second Edition, enlarged.

LONDON:
CHAPMAN AND HALL, 193 PICCADILLY.
MDCCCLXI.

LONDON :
PRINTED BY ROBSON, LEVEY, AND FRANKLYN,
Great New Street and Fetter Lane.

Preface to the Second Edition.

Messrs. Levey, Robson, and Franklyn.

GENTLEMEN,

I regret that I have not furnished you before with the enclosed additional papers, and can plead no other excuse than the usual ones, of numerous engagements, absence from home, &c. It gratifies me to learn that the first edition was so soon disposed of, and that it has been long out of print, and so often asked for. I cannot pretend to offer any judgment upon what had better be expunged from the first impression ; but the whole thing is in your hands, for you to deal with as your judgment may dictate. If you think any portion of the new matter unsuitable, I beg its rejection, and if needful I will send other extracts from Gregory's papers to replace it.

Yours faithfully,

THE SQUIRE'S SON.

Preliminary to the First Edition.

MESSRS. LEVEY AND Co. think the readers of the following pages will need no further explanation from them after perusing the annexed letters. The one signed "The Squire's Son" reached them when the work was at press, and just in time to save them the necessity of giving an introductory notice of their own.

Messrs. Levey, Robson, and Franklyn.

GENTLEMEN,
              Some years ago, my late honoured Master took me to London with him, that I might see the great show at Chiswick ; and there I got amongst a many gardeners, and some of the young ones made very merry at my old-fashioned ways ; and when I talked about getting ahead of the world, they said I'd lived in the good old times ; I couldn't do so now, if I'd my time to go over again. So, when I got home, I set to work, and put a few things down out of my books, and meant to send 'em to the gardening papers, the Chronicle or the Journal, just to tell what I've seen and done in my day ; but just then they

were squabbling about " Polmaise," and so I kept 'em ;
because I always notice, when there's a row in the
street, every body's head's out of doors or windows,
and it's hard to get attended to.   Well, they've laid
by ever since ; but now I think I'll have 'em in a
little book ; for since I've lost my honoured Master,
and he's made me easy for life with a weekly allow-
ance, I don't care spending a little money ; and so
the bearer, who is my friend,—the shopkeeper in the
village,—will hear what you say, and if it won't be too
much, he'll pay you the bill, and you may let any
body sell the book that you like.   Though I don't put
my own name and the place I live in, I know nobody
can say that I've told what isn't true ; and though
they that know me will find me out, and charge me
with writing it, I'll neither own nor deny it ; and so I
tell 'em once for all.   *I've tossed the caps down ; let
every master and man wear the one that fits him.*

Your humble servant,

JAMES GREGORY.

P.S. I shall look to you to put the papers a little
to rights when you're printing them, and to pay me
back all the booksellers can afford to give me ; and
my friend will call and see you about it next year before Christmas, when he goes to London again.

Preface to the First Edition.

To the Printers from the " Squire's Son."

GENTLEMEN,

About three weeks since, I was awakened quite early in the morning, and shocked by the information that Gregory was very ill, and supposed to be dying, and that he very much wished to see me. I directed immediately that his two daughters, who are domestics in my family, should be called ; but I learnt that they had already left the Hall for their father's cottage.

On entering the room of this worthy man, he stretched out his hand, and grasping mine with all the little power he had left him, exclaimed : "Thank you, sir ; just in time, just in time." On inquiring how long he had been ill, I was informed that, after reading a chapter in his Bible as usual, he had retired to bed in apparent good health ; but had been seized at midnight with a violent spasm of the heart, which had resisted all the apothecary's skill, and had prostrated his strength beyond every chance of recovery. I asked him if I should send for our clergyman ; but he declined, saying : " No, thank you, sir ; I want all the remainder of my time with my children. But give my duty to him, and say, one more of his flock has nearly got safe into the fold of the Great Shepherd."

I took my leave shortly afterwards, that I might not, by my presence, impose any restraint upon him or his girls ; and within a few hours afterwards I received a message to say that he was no more.

His remains were interred by the side of his wife and children ; and the unusually large number of followers and attendants at the grave gave a pleasing evidence of the respect entertained for him.

The savings of his prudent and laborious life had been disposed of by gift some time before his decease; his papers were, by his particular desire, handed over to me; and it was by this means, and from a memorandum, that I learnt he had made a selection, and placed them in your hands for publication.   I am not sure that he has chosen the best of his materials for his little work; and if it meets with a sufficient sale to warrant my doing so, I may possibly be induced, at a future time, to give some additional extracts from the quantity of observations recorded by him.   In the passage where he describes his difficulties and troubles from illness, the death of his child, &c., after losing his situation at Birdwood, he hardly does himself justice, for his conduct was manly and unexceptionable; and he was so much in request as a jobbing gardener, that my father, who never lost sight of him, and was always wishing him back again, fully believed he was doing well; and I cannot easily forget his relating to my mother how pained he had been with Mrs. Gregory's recital of their sufferings, which he had learnt from her on the day he had called at his cottage to reëngage him. My father immediately requested the apothecary to place his charge for medicine and attendance to his own account, and gave the same direction to the undertaker; but this only served to remove the surprise my father had felt at their reduced circumstances. Every farthing had been paid, and that in a manner leading them to believe that Gregory was well off. So strictly honest and just were both he and his wife, considering nothing their own if owing any one a penny.

I have no wish to make him appear in any other than his true colours; he had his faults, like all men, and entertained some violent prejudices, the effects of a very limited education; but he was a faithful servant, and withal very modest; for it was his saying, "There were plenty of better men than he, but they hadn't the masters to fetch 'em out, as he had." My father had not merely a respect for him, but a sincere regard, which his many years' faithful services had strengthened, until he occupied the place of a humble friend.

Towards the conclusion of my parent's life, when increasing infirmities prevented his usual walk to an elevated part of the grounds, where for years, when in the country, he had been accustomed to watch the setting sun decline below the horizon, Gregory was his attendant, drawing him to the spot in an easy-chair when the weather permitted. The last time my father was ever abroad in that manner I joined them, when, as usual, Gregory withdrew to a short distance;

but my father beckoned him to come back, saying, "You need not go away; we shall both of us soon be where no distinctions exist between master and man." "I never wish, sir," said his attached servant, "to be your equal any where." A tear came into my father's eye as he whistled, the signal for Gregory to draw him home.

A few days after the above occurrence, we were gathered around his bed, waiting that event which we had long dreaded, but which was then close at hand. It was the hour when Gregory was in the same attendance as when my father was able to get out. The curtains of the window were drawn aside; the sun was throwing his farewell rays upon the chamber-wall; my father looked round slowly and earnestly on the faces surrounding his bed, but with evident disappointment in his countenance. I guessed the cause, and, stepping into the passage, brought Gregory in. As soon as my father recognised him, a smile of satisfaction played about his mouth; with an effort he pointed to the window, still bright with the setting sun, gently waved his hand in farewell to us all, and immediately, his countenance assuming a look expressive of reverent surprise, he departed for a better world.

Until very lately the early riser on a Sunday morning, who might happen to be passing our little rustic church, would, on looking in at the window, have seen a tall and venerable man, mounted on a stool, carefully wiping the dust off a marble slab placed on the wall of the chancel to the memory of my father. That man was James Gregory; for such he has chosen to call himself, and his desire to remain unknown shall not be disturbed by me.

I leave it to your judgment to append this Letter to his papers or not.

I am, gentlemen,

Yours faithfully,

THE SQUIRE'S SON.

MESSRS. LEVEY AND CO.

———

A PACKET OF SEEDS

SAVED BY

AN OLD GARDENER.

MANY talk about the good old times. I remember times sixty years ago, and I can't call them good times; and if what I write is read by young gardeners, I think they'll say with me that *my times* any how, sixty years ago, were bad times. I shall never forget them till I forget my mother. She was a good poor man's wife; did for him well; fetched him from the public-house on Saturday nights; took out of his pocket what money she could find when she got him home to bed, and made the best of it. Little schooling I got; and what I did get cost nothing, and was worth less; for the master, who was too stupid for sexton and clerk of the parish, and so lost the place, made us all learn by heart what we did not understand with the head more than the hazel-stick that he thrashed us with. But if my schooling cost nothing, I can't say so of my victuals; and my mother dying, my father took more to drinking, and less found its way to the cupboard; and he was glad when a gardener, who was in our parts on a holiday, and used to drink with him, said he would get me a place under him; which he did, and to which I went, near forty miles, in a road-wagon. All my clothes went in a handkerchief-bundle, and no large one neither; and my father could ill bear to see it, for he said, "Jem," as we went to the wagon, —"Jem," said he, "take care of drink, 'tis that makes your bundle so small. Promise me that, and never learn to swear." He was a kind honest-hearted man, ruined by drink and *good fellowship*, as it was called in the "good old times."

My heart was very heavy all the way; and none the lighter when I got to my journey's end, for it was late, and my father's friend took me into a shed at the back of the green-houses, and showed me a crib of a place, where he told me I was to sleep; and giving me something to eat, said I must be tired, and had better go to bed. It was a light summer's evening; and how the birds did sing after a little rain we had! but how heavy it made my heart to be left in that place all alone! But I said the prayer my mother taught me, and in I got on the bass mats that made the mattress, with a blanket' and coverlid for bed-clothes. My wages was to be five shillings a-week, and find myself; and that was the reason, the gardener said, why I was to sleep there, because I couldn't pay for lodgings.

I was tired, and soon fell asleep, and forgot all about wages and every thing else, till a strange face called me in the morning to get up, and then I soon found out all about my new life. I was to fetch and carry from the garden to the house, sweep paths, and beat mats and carpets, and at spare times learn to dig. And these things I did many a long day; and they that recollect what a growing body and great appetite can do at the bread, let alone the beef, may guess how I felt sometimes on five shillings a-week to find all. Many a time I've seen the squire push up the dining-room window, and throw the dogs that lay about on the lawn bones that I should have been glad to pick; and

many a time I've felt queer when he has
called out to me, "Hoy! lay down your
broom, and come and take these bones off
the grass," which the dogs had done with;
and then he'd be stroking them, and saying,
"Good dog, good dog;" and they so fat and
I so lean, they so sleek and I so patchy, I
often felt quite mangy among them.   But
I'd a bold heart—my father was a pensioner
for wounds in battle—and carried my head
up as well as I could.   From the kitchen I
got nothing, except a cuff from the cook,
which she never did twice, however, for she
liked the advantage, which that time she
didn't get; but I managed pretty well, especially in hard weather, when mine and the
birds' appetites were the keenest; for then
I caught them, ay, and cooked them too;
and this was my plan : I'd pull a lot of spar-
rows, or maybe some blackbirds and thrushes,
and then cut 'em down the back, and filled
their bodies full of bread; put them in a tin
dish, cover another over them, and put the
lot pretty close up to the bars of the stoke-
hole on the top of a bank of hot ashes. When
done, and it did not take long, there was a
supper for my master, if he had but had my

appetite and my teeth, for they made bones of nothing. Two years I had of this dull work; for I'd a proud heart, and did not care to go among the boys in livery that were with the horses, for they were a bad lot; and I've noticed all my life that horses seem to spoil any body that has much to do with them, whether master or man.

These boys were a terrible plague to the only friend I seemed to have in the world that wore a petticoat; they were always tormenting her, and calling her a witch; and they had nearly persuaded me that she was one, too, when she first took me up. She'd lost her husband not long before I came; and having nobody else to scold, she seemed glad of me to keep her tongue in tune; and yet in a little while I found it was only a habit of hers, and a cover to a deal of real kindness. One while she'd scold me for not being clean; another time because my clothes were dirty or ragged; and then she'd scrub my head or neck, or wash my linen, or put a patch here and a darn there; and take so little of my money for doing it, that she was another mother to me for these matters.

This poor woman's work was weeding in the garden and shrubbery walks, or sometimes round the plantation hedges; and what with sun and wind and old age, she was like a shrivelled apple, with a little red colour left in its cheeks. The only place she could go to for dinner was the shed where I slept; and there, over the stoke-hole, we used to sit and eat together; and many's the tale of trouble that poor creature's told me, especially in winter, when we were both of us the worst off. If it hadn't been for her I'm sure I should have gone off to sea, or for a drummer-boy, spite of the horrid tales I'd heard my father's old comrades tell about the wars, when they used to be drinking together after they'd drawn their pension-money. And talking of that, I've never read of any bloody murders to match things I've heard some of 'em boast of doing, and glory in, too. Not my father, he was the wrong sort of man; and often, after I'd been listening, he would say, "Bad work, boy, bad work; and who's to account for it by and by I don't know; but I hope not me, though I've had so much to do with it."

And I must say that, to this day, I can't
quite see how that which is so dreadfully
wicked for a man to do, to serve his own
ends, can be any thing else but wicked when
it's done for some trumpery little quarrel
between one country and another, such as
I've read about in histories. But I must
not forget this poor old woman. I've said
the stable-boys called her a witch; and to
prove it, they said the cats would always
get about her if they .could, and she could
handle snakes without their hurting her;
and one boy said he once caught her with
a great ugly toad feeding out of her hand.
At last the kettle got too hot to hold the
water, and blew the lid off; for all the horses
were taken bad together; and the coachman
complained to the squire that it was all because he had offended the old woman, and
she had bewitched 'em.

The squire, for fun, I suppose, called old
Mary to book; but she soon showed him
that it was because she gave the cats mice
and little birds that they purred about her;
and if she handled snakes, it was only the
harmless sorts, and not vipers. About the
toad she amused him a good deal, by fetch-

ing a handful of tan out of one of the pits that was full of sow-bugs; and bringing him out of the flower-pot he lived in, she put it before him; and, as the squire said, he stood like his pointers would have done at a pheasant, only turning his bright eye, and sending out his long tongue and licking the sow-bugs up with a click, one after the other, before they could run out of his reach, and never missing one. It taught me a lesson, if it didn't any body else,—and that was, to look into things myself, and not take all for granted people say; and I believe, if all of us that are gardeners did this, we should find many things we think bad, like little birds, frogs, toads, efts, lizards, and snakes, too, are good things in their places.

I was glad to find my old friend come off so well; for I couldn't have borne to have stopped where I was without her; and we went on very comfortably together till she died, when for a while it was like losing my mother again, I was so very lonely.

Let all young gardeners set great store by a good mother; they can have but one, and if that one be but such as mine was, they have a blessing. What would have become of my poor father and my two sisters and myself if it hadn't been for her I cannot tell. She was always at work; and drink as my father would, she never nagged him, and often coaxed him out of the public-houses, and persuaded him at times to stop at home. If she could not find him when he was out tippling, she always would sit up for him to let him in. She brought up my two sisters to house-work, and got them places in good families; and they kept them, always bettering themselves when they changed; and they sent home many a pound to help keep a house over our parents' heads. Masters and mistresses little think how some servant-girls help their old or sick parents and brothers and sisters. They often say, " The girls might save if they would; but they don't believe they lay by a penny." I have known a pretty many that have denied themselves a good deal, and my eldest sister was one of them. She would not marry till my father died, though her sweetheart promised to keep him. " No," said she; " if there comes a family, then there's nothing but the workhouse for him. My sisters had me home, and gave me a

suit of black for his funeral, and we had a
few days together again. Our next meeting will be in heaven, I expect; for they
had no schooling, and I was a poor writer,
and letters cost eightpence a piece for post-
age; so that the sight of one almost frightened me when I was so poor. I have heard
they both married, and after a while went to
America. They were both nice singers, and
father and mother and we three have had
many a pleasant evening with our harmony;
for it wonderfully helps to bind up a family
does a little simple music and singing together.

But a change in my hard kind of life was
oddly brought about. One November night
I was fast asleep, when I woke and thought
the world was come to an end. .A furious
gust of wind had blown the top off a great
elm that hung over the furnace-shed where I
slept, and crushed in one end of the roof,
smashed the glass of the greenhouse, and
ruined the whole concern. This worked my
deliverance; for the squire, coming with my
lady to look at the mischief in the morning,
saw my crib, and said, "What's that hole
for?" (His sporting dogs' kennel was a

beauty to it.) I was by, and answered, "It's my bed-place, sir." "The —— it is !" said he. "Why didn't you complain to me about it ?" I began to tell him that I had once asked for a little more wages, when he had only said, "That be ——." But before I had said as much he moved away. Now he was not a bad-hearted man, but he never looked into such things as he did into things about his dogs and horses; and if he used foul language, in "the good old times," I suppose, it was thought "the thing." This I know, every man and boy about the premises did the same, and tried to improve upon it; and that's another thing I've learnt, that let servants try to imitate "their betters" in any thing else, they were always beat; but at swearing and the like Jack was as good as gentleman ; and if nothing else didn't make the quality leave off the habit, I wonder that didn't; for such-like persons as our squire like to see a distinction as much as any of the florists.

In the afternoon the butler came to me, and said I was to go and lodge at a cottage on the green. It belonged to our master, and he let a widow-woman live in it rent-free,

because her husband, who was once coachman in the family, was killed by one of the
horses flinging him at exercise. The butler
was to give me the offer of a place, too, in the
stable, and out of livery; but I begged off,
for I did not like stable ways; and I knew
that at exercise before breakfast the coachman and grooms always had something to
drink at a public-house they passed by; and
I hadn't then forgot what my father said at
parting about drinking, and its making my
bundle so small. So I begged off; and when
I told the reason, the butler said I was a
great fool, for " what harm did a glass do a
man?" and yet all the while his nose and
face were giving the lie to his tongue.

After work I went to my lodgings; and
queer enough I felt when I went in with my
bundle of little better than rags, for I'd my
best on my back. I hadn't the heartiest of
welcomes. The old lady did washing for the
Hall servants, and the cottage wasn't the
largest. She had two sons; one was coachman to the squire, and one a servant somewhere else; and she had one daughter, who
helped at home. This girl was two years
older than me, and so marked with the small-

pox, that the other girls in the village used
to call her "Pock-pitted Bet." You never
saw any of them keep company with her in
going to church (she kept no holidays);
she was so plain, and she dressed so plain,
too, and so neat. And there was something
in that; for any body that passed her and
looked back at her face wasn't disappointed
at all. It's often set me wondering how
ordinary people can be so foolish as to dress
so fine, and sometimes outrageously grand,
as if to call people to look at their want of
beauty; and many a laugh I've seen at some
of the Hall folks on this score. And not at
the Hall folks only, for I've often seen the
same at other people : if you looked at the
things on their backs, and their airs, you'd
surely have taken them for quality; and if
you only watched 'em long enough, you'd see
'em slip into some little poking place, and
no occasion to walk in after them to see if
it was clean and all to rights; for I always
noticed, that when people make themselves
so fine for the sake of being looked at,
they're sure to spend a deal of time looking
at other people. Somebody goes by the
window, up they jump; and that look's not

enough, they must go to the door, or to the
bedroom up-stairs; and if they once get
their elbows on the window-sill, no more
hearty work that day. But Elizabeth was
none of this sort, and though she was so
common-looking in her face and dress, and,
as I said, none of the other girls kept her
company, yet I always noticed, that when
any of them were in any trouble (and they
were safe to be after our young gentlemen
had been home from college), they were sure
to find their way to her to make her their
friend.

But what's all this to do with flowers or
gardening? Wait a bit, and you shall see;
and if young gardeners cannot learn a lesson
from what I've noticed, they can't do what
I did. That first evening I went in, I sat
still and out of the way, till I saw the old
woman going for some wood to make up the
fire for her irons (she and her daughter were
ironing), when up I got, and fetched it for
her; and after a while, and some supper, I
went to bed, — and such a bed! after my
hole in the shed, it was like a nobleman's to
me. Next morning, when I went to work,
I was told by the head-gardener that the

young man above me was gone into the
stable, and I was to have his place, and ten
shillings a-week, out of which I was to pay
one shilling and sixpence a week to the
widow for lodging and washing. This was
a fine lift for me in all ways; for now I was
to work in the houses as well as the grounds.
Three months only I had in this place before
the under-gardener left, and I got his situation. And now I found the use of having
amused myself in reading and writing; for
I had for a long time before put down every
night what I had seen done or done myself
in the day (though it was in a poor way of
writing to be sure), and this helped me wonderfully.

The head-gardener was a kind man, and
took as great pains to teach me as I did to
learn. He was no one's enemy but his own,
only in one way, and that was his example,
which was bad for others. He must have
had a good temper once; but his drinking
habits killed all his respect for himself, and
then he forgot his respect for others, and was
very violent to his under men. I was eight
years with him, and did all I could to keep
things straight; but the more I did the

worse he got; for when he found things
done, he kept more away from his duty, till
things went back for want of help, and matters got very unpleasant indeed. Just as
they were about the worst, I got another
place, and that all in a hurry. I'd often
wondered if ever I should better myself;
and just when I had least hope, I got what
I wanted, without asking.

One day a friend of my master's was
walking round with him, and just as they
came where I was nailing some wall-trees,
the gentleman said, "I want a good gardener;
does your man know one?" "There's one,"
said the squire; " you may have him, if you
like." A few words settled it, and I was to
go in a month upon trial. I don't know
what else my master said, but I did hear
him say, "He's a methodistical fellow, and
that'll just suit you."

It was the fashion fifty years ago to call
any body a methodist that kept decent, and
didn't go to church. The methodists had
turned an old barn outside the village into
a meeting-house, and a good many poor people used it, and very angry it made the parson and the gentry; but they took an odd

way to put it down, for they would give
none of the charities to such as went to hear
the preacher, nor let them have any of the
allotments. It mattered not how good the
people were, go to church they must, or nothing for them ; but let a man be ever such
a blackguard, if he did but go to the church,
he got the coals and bread and allotment. All
this was no use, it only made folks like a
spiteful donkey at a hedge,—be as sharp as
you will about him, there's his heels ready
for you. Some labourers got discharged because they would go to meeting, and that
made martyrs of them, but a poor kind; for
if it hadn't been for the notice they got,
and being made something of, they'd soon
have gone to church again of their own ac-
cord. Two things I noticed, and I've always
found it the same every where :

> " When the parson goes much to the Hall,
> The poor parishioners go to the wall ;
> And when a labourer's made a deacon,
> It always spoils his stomach for bacon."

A word or two more, and I've done about
this matter. If the Church of England minis-
ters would only save seed more carefully, and
sow it more industriously, they'd see a deal

better crops; and if we poor folks only *talked* religion less, and *did* religion more, we shouldn't hear so much sneering at meetingers.

About a week after I got engaged, my old landlady died very suddenly, which was a great blow to her daughter, for it turned her upon the world; but she got lodgings, and the promise of the same washing, and the house was to be given up when I went away; and till then an aunt came to stop with Elizabeth. She and her mother had been all along very kind to me; and when the day came for me to go, it seemed another leaving home, for I had looked so long at that face, that I knew every pockmark upon it. I helped get her washing-tubs, lines, and things to her new home, and then bid her good-bye. I thought I saw a tear when she said, " I wish you well, or I would not say, Don't you be caught by Margaret."

I went off rather affronted at this, saw Margaret and some more, and started for my new place, near eighty miles off. It was morning when I got there, and early, so I had a good look round, and found every thing very badly done: all was slovenly

and dirty, and at sixes and sevens, and yet
there was a good deal for that part and
those days; there was a conservatory,
greenhouse, and pits, with two houses of
grapes. It was November, and not a
flower. As soon as my new employer was
up, I was ordered in. He first asked me
how I liked the look of things, and I told
him very well indeed. He said he was glad
of that; his old gardener that had died was
"a very clever fellow," and he hoped I
should be as good. And I've heard this
same said many a time since by gentlemen
over as stupid fellows as ever robbed a *real
gardener* of a place. He told me, in a way
I was quite strange to, that he wished to
see every body about him happy and comfortable, and that he must have no quarrelling; and if those under me did not behave
as I wished, I was to tell them civilly, and
if they did not mend then, to bring them
before him. He said I must join a benefit-
club that the clergyman managed, and try
and save something beside. "And mind,"
said he, "though you are upon trial, what
you are at first is your own pattern, and I
must have all the piece like it." He then

told me to go to the butler, and have my
breakfast in the servants' hall. It *was* a
hall to the one I'd left; for though I never
eat in that one, I knew those that did by
heart, and pleased enough I was to see the
difference. I don't mean that my new ac-
quaintances were extraordinary, not a bit
of it; only there was something about 'em
that made you feel comfortable, and they
had no stupid airs.

Now here's another thing that's no rid-
dle, and yet I'll set it for an answer. How
do you account for some hall-porters and
livery and other servants being so saucy to
decent people in some places, when in
others, ay, and very often where there's
real rank too, all the servants are so civil
and respectful? I've seen so much of·*this*,
that let me see the servants, and I'll tell
you what the masters and mistresses are
without seeing *them*.

I soon got to work; and the weather
being bad, and the squire (this was squire
as well as the last) not able to get out, I
had a good chance to alter things a little.
I began upon the greenhouse—washed the
glass and paint-work outside: this made a

better light to get the plants cleaned; and a pretty job it was to get the scale off and the fly killed. It was long since they'd smelt tobacco. I had a foreman, two men, and a boy; and a good set they were, only at first humdrum and sleepy, like him that was gone before me. After the plants were got in as good order as they could be, a few lumps of lime slacked in water served to whiten the wall and flue; and a sponge, brush, and mop altered the inside of the paint-work as much as the out. When we had finished, my foreman said, "I would not have believed it." We did just the same with the vineries; and when they were finished, I made my men clean themselves; for I always say, that a gardener that does not keep his body and clothes clean is a dirty gardener with his plants; and if I was a gentleman, I'd have nobody about me that neither pleased eyes nor nose.

I had a comfortable pretty little cottage on the premises, and that's where a gardener should be. One nice room opened on to the garden, and that was fitted up for my master and the ladies. An elderly woman did for me and the boy, who slept in the cottage, as I was not married. She worked, too, a little in the garden, and every little was a help then, for there was every thing to do except the kitchen-garden; that was in order. There was not a mould-heap—nothing to hand, all to make. It was tight work, I assure you. There was the cow-man to please, for the cart that brought fodder for his yard was the only one I could get. Then there was the keeper on the look-out to pick a hole in my coat about disturbing his game when I went in the woods for leaf-mould; and the coachman, he would not half muck his stables out, for he said he wanted his horses to lay warm, and so had clean straw over a foot of dung. Clipping wasn't the fashion then. When they all said 'no' to my wants, I said, "Very well," and thanked 'em; and 'no' they said a long while, but yet I thanked 'em, till I fairly tired 'em out into saying 'yes;' and as I showed myself ready to oblige them, they soon took to obliging me. People can stand quarrelling with all their lives; it's like whetting your scythe with your rubber,— the longer you do it the sharper it gets; but they can't stand good nature; let 'em

be ever so cross, they're sure to give in,
like the same scythe against moss.   The
keeper was the worst, and they always are.
Kind, good man as our squire was, the game
seemed to lie nearer his heart than any thing
else.   That's often been another puzzler to
me, how gentlemen that are justices of
peace can keep so much temptation for the
poor man as a head of game, when they see
every week and every sessions what comes
of it.   Then look at Mr. Keeper: if the
tenants didn't please him, they couldn't call
the farm their own, for he'd watch for some
flaw about 'em as he'd watch a poacher, and
he'd have 'em out by hook or crook.   But I
got the right side of him too, and in a little
while had my mould-heaps all to hand, well
turned over, frosted, and housed.

I brought some things with me, and a
few neighbouring gardeners helped me to a
few more, and I made the best of a little.
I noticed, that whenever my master or mistress came into the garden, it was only to
walk, not to look in the houses, which they
didn't come near.   Christmas - day came
round ; and when my lady came into the
breakfast-room, I contrived that she should

find a basket of forced flowers; poor things to be sure, but enough for what I wanted. Christmas time was not kept at the Hall, except by the in-door servants; all the out-door ones had beef, and things for puddings, for my lady said she thought wives and children ought to have their share.

When the Christmas party was all gone, the squire and his lady were walking one day as usual, when they left the terrace and came to the houses, and went through them; and my master said, "Have you got all you want, gardener?" Now that was the very thing I wanted. When men go to new places, they often frighten their employers by saying they must have this and that and the other, instead of doing their best with what they find. I told him I should be glad of a few things, and he gave me orders to get them. I could tell that he saw the money wouldn't be thrown away, though he said nothing of the kind. My lady said a word or two about the pretty flowers I'd sent in, and noticed what I'd been doing about their garden-room front. But I'd watched, and seen that their eyes were not idle in the houses, and I heard, too, when they were going away, "New brooms sweep clean." "Ay," thought I, "and so will the old stump, if you only put it to the right kind of work."

I found I'd a comfortable place of it; and now and then a brother gardener would call in, for I didn't go about much, and in particular when the family was away, though then's a leisure time. But evenings in winter seemed long; and one day a neighbouring gardener asked me if I'd go to the King's Head on a Wednesday evening, and smoke a pipe with a few more that met in a friendly way. I didn't think much about it, and said I would; and yet before that time, and I don't know why, I wished I hadn't agreed. However, as I'd promised, I thought I'd go and see what it was like; and if it didn't please me, I needn't keep it up.

It was a cold February evening when I walked to the King's Head; and, I believe you, it was a pleasant sight, the great fire, and clean sanded floor, and well-rubbed tables, with clean pipes and screws of tobacco, and a box, that when a penny was dropped in opened its lid, and said, "Fill away; but shut down tight, or pay another penny." One dropped in after another, till all were together; when I was *colted*, as they called it, and put in the chair, for which I had to stand treat. One meeting was a fair sample of all; we had a deal of business, as there always is at such times, minding other people's and neglecting our own. It was wonderful how wise we were about our masters, and all that went on in their families; then we'd talk about the affairs of the parish and the nation, and as to the Parliament house, it was a fool to us; and I believe we talked and smoked and drank ourselves into the belief that there was but a few folks that knew any thing, and they were to be found at the King's Head any Wednesday evening. One thing I wondered at, and that was, where the money came from to pay for mixed liquors, which some called for. I know my pocket was getting very bare, and that very fast; for where I never had any thing to drink but at meals, now I wanted half a pint for lunch, and half a pint at four o'clock; and I often found myself saying, "It's only half a pint," excusing myself like to myself. I often remembered my poor father, and his last words; but then I

thought I should never get like him, and
kill myself with it as he'd done. But now
I think I should soon have been just such
another poor slave to drink, only one morning the squire pulled me up short with,
" Well, gardener, you and the King's Head
are too well acquainted to please me." At
first, I was for making some excuse; but he
stopped that very short, and said, " You can
do as you like, and I can do the same. You
may choose the public-house for your evenings, and I can choose a man that spends his
time at home ; but let me tell you, whether
with me or in another place, you'll find bad
habits like your flower-pots,—you may break
'em, but you'll never wear 'em out;". and
then he left me.

My eye was opened, and I turned over
a new leaf, and left the King's Head altogether; for which I got called a few hard
names, but they spoil no meat. I must say,
that at first I used to sneak off if I saw any
of my old companions; for somehow or other
I couldn't stand being twitted with, " He's
afraid of his master," and the like. Before
I took the place, the old gardener always
paid the quarterly bills ; but now they were

paid at the house: but when the squire found I was always in my cottage of an evening, he sent me to pay the tradesmen; and then I found out how it was that the mixed liquors were paid for. There was the glazier took the money, and offered me a shilling in the pound; and so with them all. They said it was the custom. "But," said I, "does the squire know it?" "No," said they, "nor has no business to." Well, I didn't want to make myself out over-honest; but yet I couldn't help thinking that, if it was any body's, it was my master's. Then I thought, "If I speak to the squire, it will make trouble, so I'll think it over." When I was ordered to take my book in, I took courage, though I didn't like the job, and asked if he allowed me to take poundage. He seemed rather bothered at first; but when I told him what I meant, he said, "Gardener, take it now, and I'll talk to you about it another time." And so he did, and gave me *twenty pounds* a-year more wages, and told me always after that, at buying, to do as well for him as I should for myself; and tell the tradesmen that it was not to be paid by them any more. And so he did with the butler and the coachman; and we all liked it, for they said there always seemed something underhand about it;—and so there is too, and I wonder masters don't know better, and pay fair good wages, and do away with these things. 'Tisn't in human nature to make bills small, when the larger they are the better for him that pays them.   It can't be expected that a man that gives nothing shall get orders, when another man allows poundage.   Give good full wages, say I, and you'll get the best of servants, or else change them.

After a while I asked the squire for a holiday, to go and see my friends at the old place; and when he said "Yes," he told me he should not find fault if I got a wife, provided she was the right sort; for he said it didn't look well for a man to live single when he'd a comfortable place, and was a little ahead of the world.   I'd thought the same thing; and, to tell the truth, that was just what I wanted the holiday for.

Old friends at the old place shook hands very hearty ; and Margaret, with all her fine clothes, hadn't forgotten me ; and when we shook hands, hers was so soft, I could but look at it, and so white it was and so small, that it set me thinking a deal more than I care to tell; but this I did, I went a few miles, and bought a golden hoop to have a leap through.

"You might have called before this," said Elizabeth, "to see an old friend," as I opened her door one evening. "I saw you pass; and I did think you'd have looked in."

I made some excuse, and we sat down, and talked over old times, over those dead and gone, and those still about; and we felt more like brother and sister than any thing else. She told me all her troubles—how hard she had to work, and how she'd lost part of the washing at the Hall through the lady's-maid, though she couldn't learn why, only it was so; and then she said she meant to go to service; and if I should hear of any thing likely to suit her, she'd thank me to let her know: she wasn't afraid of work, only she wanted to be comfortable,—for she wasn't at all so as things were.

"Well," said I, "I know just the place for you, if you'll take it; but you'll have to work hard and live hard, and sometimes

have to put up with a good deal; for the
master's an obstinate man, and, right or
wrong, he will have his way."

"I don't mind that," said she, "if I can
but be comfortable, and be let do my work;
—but you'll see me again before you go,
and then you can tell me more about it;"
and she put out her hand, and said, "Good-
bye."

"But," said I, "there's no hurry; this
hard hand of yours has done enough for to-
day;" and I slipped the ring on her finger,
and said, "If you're of my mind, we'll make
another move with the old washing-tubs
and the lines and the pegs; and for fear
you lose the place, say you'll take it, and
I'll soon show you the way."

'Tisn't worth telling; for nothing's easier
than getting married, if you go the right
way about it. And though the girls in the
village said I was taking her home to scare
the birds off my seeds, I knew what I'd got,
and so did they, and none better than Margaret. But the less said the better; only
I'd have young men know, that there's more
truth than they think for in the old saying,
"Fine feathers make fine birds." Ay, too

fine by half; and 'tisn't till they're fixed
for life that they find out how often " a silk
sock hides a sore toe."

How the squire and his lady did giggle
when they saw the wife I'd brought home,
though they did all they could to hide it,
and turn it off on something else! " Let
them laugh that wins," thought I; though
I did feel vexed, I must allow. But they
were a pattern of a master and mistress; no
looking down upon those Providence had
placed under them,—always a kindly look
or word for all that behaved themselves;
but if there was any thing wrong, then look
out; there was to go into master's room,
and such a lecture—he was like a counsel-
lor. Dear me, if employers would but talk
a little more, in a kindly way, to their people, how many wrong notions would be got
rid of! Why, there isn't one master in a
hundred knows any thing about what goes
on in a man's mind,—how it rankles in their
hearts to see a sick horse or a lame dog sat
up with! while, if he's bad, he may lie at
home, and never so much as a kindly message. Yet it's all for want of thought; for
there's a deal lost by it. A kind heart's

like getting into a cold bed in a winter's
night; if you warm the sheets first, there's
the blankets underneath to warm you in
return; and so it is with poor men: if
you're frightened at the first chill, you'll
never find the glow there is about them,
that only wants fetching out. I hate to
hear some say, "The poor are so ungrateful." Look now, people give away some
coals in winter-time, or some clothes to poor
women,—and some mean well enough, ay,
and do such things and let nobody know it;
but if it wasn't for seeing their names in
print, and it's being a public subscription,
five out of ten wouldn't give sixpence. Well,
perhaps, by and by these same people want
a job done for one shilling that's worth two
shillings and sixpence; and then comes the
cry, "Poor people are so ungrateful." Out
on such charity! say I.

And now let me tell about a bit of my
foolishness; for I've been foolish, like my
father before me, though maybe in a different way. I feel ashamed of it; but perhaps
the telling it may help some young men to
keep out of the pit I fell into, and teach 'em
when they've got a good place to try and

keep it; for I've learnt—ay, and bitterly, too, once in my life—that if good men are scarce, good places are not like hedge-fruit in autumn. I've heard men, when they've got discharged, and been a bit fuddled, say : "I don't care; more places than parish-churches." That "don't care" saying does a deal of harm, for men use it till they believe it; and very often, when they say it loudest they care the most; but young people catch the word, and soon find the trouble "don't care" brings. But I'm forgetting my story. I was now a sober man, a steady man; and as to work, it never frightened me. I was always at it; and the squire saw this, and left things in the gardens and grounds pretty much to me. People saw this; and where they used to call me James or Gregory, now they called me "Mr. Gregory." The Bible says true enough, "Pride goeth before destruction, and a haughty spirit before a fall." I began to take on; and if the squire gave me any orders, I did not take 'em as I ought to have done. If he had a plan, I had a plan; if he wanted any thing done, I was just going to do it, *only* something or other; and then I was often saying, at such times, "I'm sure I'm always at work ; I do the best I can ;" and the like. I little thought what was coming, and all of a sudden too. One evening, when I went in as usual with my book at the end of the month, after the squire had looked it over, he turned full to me, and, lifting his spectacles off his nose, said : " Gardener, I wish you to get another place ; I give you a month's notice, and I'll give you a month's pay beside ; but in a month the man I've taken on will be here. You want your way in every thing, and I'll have my own. If you do all you can, you are always telling me so ; and I want a man that'll recollect that I do my part too." My eyes flew open like a pair of window-shutters, and I saw all as clear as if I'd just come out of a wood: but it was no use asking him to let me stay with him ; he heard all I had to say, but still the same answer, " My new man will be here in a month."

I never shall forget my walk back to the cottage, nor all I felt when I told my wife that I was to go, and when I looked at the children as they lay asleep in their little beds. I couldn't read the chapter in the

Bible that night, as I always used to do; but my wife took the book, and said, "The more trouble, the more need of something to mend it." But, poor thing, her voice was so choky, I couldn't have understood her if I'd listened, which I couldn't do at all.

Time never went faster than it did that black month. I couldn't hear of any place; or, if I did, I couldn't get it; for 'twas not easy to get one after leaving our squire. People always thought there must be something wrong, though I showed a good character from him; and at last I was obliged to turn out of my happy home into a bit of a cottage in the village. I made it as late as I could before we went in; and how strangely I did feel, as the children ran up and down the rickety old stairs, so pleased with a new place; and the canary sung so loud, whilst our hearts were so heavy! Next morning I got up early, and dug up the bit of garden, and put that to rights, and tied in the honeysuckle in front of the house; and my wife, she cleaned the windows, and made all as tidy as we could; for we wanted people to see that we weren't idle folks, though I was out of place. I let the little shopkeeper know too, and asked him to tell others for me, that I was willing to do a job for any body till I got another situation; and so I got jobbing-work here and there, in gardens or at trees, with the farmers, and other people that didn't keep regular gardeners. But no one knows how my heart ached to see our little savings going, and my wife wearing down with work and illness among the children; for they took ill about three months after I lost my place, and kept so a long time; and when one died, it came so heavy to think it might be all owing to our poor house and living; and I took up hard feelings against the squire, for what I thought was cruel in him to discharge me as he did; as if he hadn't as much right to choose a man as I had to choose a place, or how to behave in it. I think I could have done, if it hadn't been for sickness, for we lived very close; but at last we had spent our little club-money, and were obliged to ask a little credit. That we had never done before! and now we found out what a miserable thing it is; for when the debt got a little larger, instead of less, my wife told me she noticed the shopkeeper

D

served other people before her, though she
came first, and had been waiting; asking
them what they'd please to want, but letting her ask for herself.   My heart was as
proud as ever, and couldn't bear this; so
one morning I took a few little silver things
I had, and told the grocer to keep them till
I could fetch them away, and pay him; but
I dare say he thought that would never be,
for he knew we were going down hill.   And
one of my windows got broke, and had a
sheet of paper pasted over it, and there's no
poorer look than that; and glad I was afterwards it was broke,—as I shall tell, just to
show how one good turn deserves and gets
another.

Time wore away, and I did as well as I
could.   Once I had got a few days' work at
a farmer's some way off, and had to get up
early, and was late getting home; and I
wasn't quite as strong as I used to be.   At
this farmer's I always had my meals given
me, and I managed to save a bit to bring home
for my wife and the children.   I left one
very ill one morning, my only boy; and
when I got home at night he was very bad.
I never found my wife in such trouble

before; and when we looked at his poor
worn face and bony hands, and then when
our eyes met one another, I thought no two
people on earth could be more miserable.
I noticed, as I got in, the broken window
was mended; and so, for something to talk
about, and turn our thoughts a bit, I spoke
about it. "Oh," said my wife, "I forgot
to tell you that George came and put it in,
and said he'd do any other little thing for
us like that, and be glad of it." This George
was a poor outcast of a boy that I'd got the
painter and glazier to take, when it was
worth his while to please me; and he'd behaved well, and got on, and made himself a
workman and useful. And while I was out
he'd walked down, and asked my wife to
let him mend the broken square; for he said
I'd made a man of him, and he'd never forget it while he could handle a diamond; and
before he'd see our window go broken, he'd
go without a day's victuals. It almost made
me whimper to see this bit of sunshine, when
every thing else looked so cloudy.

It was late in summer, and I was up
early next morning and off to my work, got
it done, and went into the house to get my

supper and my money, for they paid me at this house every day. "I haven't got your two shillings for you," said the maid; "for master and mistress went out, and I suppose forgot it." She saw me turn colour a bit, I dare say, for she said, "I can let you have it out of my own money, if you like;" but I hastily said, "No, thank you;" and putting my supper in my basket, went off home. My way was through a field, with a roundish hill and a plantation in it, and the paths went right and left from the stile to the two ends of the village; and the right-hand one was my proper track. I never went the other way, for it took me past my old happy home, and I couldn't bear the sight of it. Things never looked worse than they did this evening; for I thought of my home, and my sick boy, and my quite empty pocket. Why I did it, I can't tell, but I took the left-hand path this time, and struck up to the side of the plantation that looked right down on the cottage. It was empty, for the man that got my place was gone; and the clergyman, when he told us he was going away, once when he came to see our sick boy, said that the squire had told him he'd engaged another, and that before I could have asked him to take me on again. I sat down, as much out of sight in the hedge of the plantation as I could; the workmen were all gone home, and the windows were open to let the paint dry, for it was being done up all through. The roses, honeysuckle, and the jasmine, that I had planted, were all unnailed and laid down for them to nail fresh bark upon the uprights and over the porchway. I felt as if my heart would burst as I looked at it and the garden beyond; and I stopped and stopped, for the more I remembered my home there, the more I dreaded going to the one in the village.

I don't know how long I'd been there, when I heard a rustling, and directly after out came the squire's favourite retriever, and he just behind him, out of a little gate to a private path through the plantation. He saw me in a minute as I jumped up, and said, "Is that you, Gregory?" I tried to lift my hat; but whether my sad thoughts had made my forehead swell, or what it was, I couldn't move it; and I turned my head away, for I didn't want him to see all my face would have shown him,—for I'd been

thinking he might as well have given me
the place again as have taken on a stranger;
and I thought, too, he might as well have
let me earn the little things his lady often
sent to my wife, for they were very kind,
and gave us many little nice things for the
sick children we couldn't have bought.

When I got in, I found the boy better,
and the young ladies and their governess had
been to the cottage, and somehow cheered
up my wife; for when I told her I had an
empty pocket, she tried to cheer me up too,
and said, "Why, Gregory, never mind; if
'tis winter with us now, spring'll come by
and by. You never knew the longest night
without a morning; if we've care now, comfort'll come in time; so let's hope on." It
did me good to hear her; but afterwards I
laid it to her having had a present of a new
warm shawl and stout pair of shoes, which
the young ladies' governess had given her;
and about her I'll have a word to say before
I've done, for I've learnt a little about other
people beside gardeners, though I've been
one all my life.

Though I've told all my troubles, I
wouldn't have young gardeners think I was

a chicken-hearted, snivelling kind of fellow: through 'em all I walked stiff and upright; I never put my nose in another man's pot, and never begged a favour of a living soul. Pinched as I was, nobody knew it but my partner; and badly as we were off, all was as tidy as a new pin; she'd have no rags nor dirt, no reminding me what we once had been, and what I'd lost; and if our sick children hadn't kept her at home, she'd never have wanted a day's charing, for she was a favourite with gentle and simple, and in the worst of times was always ready to help a poor sick neighbour; and every body had a kindly word for her when they saw her homely face.

The day after I met the squire, I was coming down the path home, and when just in sight of the cottage I met the young ladies and their governess, as I often did, and very kindly I thought they all spoke to me as they struck off to the other pathway for the gate by my old garden cottage, which they used to go home by. The nearer my house I got, the more I stared; the bit of blind was took away from the window, and it was wide open, and somehow it looked

very strange; and the women neighbours
were standing gossiping in a lot together.
I couldn't make it out, and most of all when
I got in and found the place as empty as an
egg-shell. Nobody was there, only a boy,
who gave me a little note and walked out
directly; and this is what it said, and it almost took my breath away to read it:

"JAMES GREGORY,—If you like to go
back to your old cottage, you are welcome to
do so; and it will be your own fault if you
ever have to leave it again. You will find
your good wife and your children there. I
wish to see all about me happy and comfortable, and the way for you to be so is, to let
me be master and you be man. If you think
so too, go back to Birdwood again."

I need not tell how quick I was off, and
how often I said, and how heartily, "Thank
God!" I was soon there. And what a happy
sight! the window-blind just enough of one
side to show the old table in the old spot, all
laid out and ready, as if I had never moved
away at all; and inside there was my sick
boy in his chair, and the two little girls, and
dicky's cage on its old nail, and every bit of
furniture in its place; and the little corner

mahogany cupboard, with its glass front and little silver things that I had left with the shopkeeper, that was back too.

"How's this, mother?" I said to my wife; "how's this?" But, poor thing, she couldn't speak; and so to tea we went; but, do what I would, I couldn't swallow a bit to eat, only a cup or two; and I was off and on my seat so often, and here and there to look at things, I was just like a chip in an eddy. After tea, I set to work and got the bedsteads put together, and things up-stairs all to rights; and when the children were laid down, I had my wife tell me all about how it was I'd got back. It was not the new shawl and shoes made her so cheerful the evening before; but the squire had been down whilst I was out, and told her I was to be his gardener again; but that she wasn't to say a word to me about it, for he did not want me to know; and he'd send the cart and take all the things up to the cottage, and she was to go up and make all as comfortable as she could before I got back from my work. When she thanked him, she was like all womenfolks, she out with all our troubles, and what we'd suffered one way and another;

and would have kept on for an hour, I dare say, only the squire blew his nose so loud to stop her, as she thought, and bid her not say a word to me, only do as he bid. " And," said he, " if you are glad he should live with me again, you may thank Miss Laura, the governess ; for I always thought Gregory was doing very well, till she told me he was not, and then I meant him to come back when my gardener left; and I would have told him so when I saw him up against the plantation, only he did not seem to care to speak to me." " That shows," said I, " how people don't understand one another, all for want of a word or two. If he'd only have said he wanted to speak to me, how glad I should have been to have heard him say as much as he did to you !"

Gardeners, like other people, think they are worse off than every body else; and when they see fine clothes, and fine houses and horses, and the like, they fancy them that have them must be happy. So listen to this.

Before I lost my place, one stormy November evening, about eight o'clock, we were sitting by the fire, when there came a knock

at the door. I took the light, and had
hardly turned the lock and handle, when
open it blew, out went the candle, and in
came, with the wind and rain, a young lady,
asking shelter. We soon had her in by the
fire; and, poor thing, what a figure—so wet
and so draggled! With it all, she put on
a deal of airs, and talked about being used
to ride in a carriage, not being used to get
wet, and the like. My wife gave me a hint,
and so I took my lantern, put on my coat,
and off into the houses to see all right, as
every gardener should do before he goes to
bed. A drop of candle-grease here and
there, now and then, always pleased me
when I saw it in a morning, as it showed
my foreman had had a look-out for a slug or
something the evening before. Well, the
rain cleared off and the moon shone out;
and when I got in-doors again the lady was
gone.

"Poor thing," said my wife, "she's the
governess at the Grange House, and been
brought up a lady, and yet she's so thin of
clothes, and so proud, I could hardly get her
to put on my thick shawl and a pair of my
shoes and stockings to go home in, though

she'd catch her death of cold to keep those on that's by the fire. I did get her to, with some coaxing, poor thing, though she sobbed as if her heart would break when I wrapped her up well and made her comfortable, and saw her into the village."

A few evenings after this, she came again, and brought back my wife's things. We were sitting round the table, and our little boy was drawing in his way to amuse himself, and had got a sprig of jasmine. She didn't seem in any hurry to go, but took her bonnet off, and sat down with us, and took his pencil, and showed him how to make it look more natural, and said, if he would like to learn, she should like to teach him a little; and she drew him a stalk, with a leaf and flower, and bid him copy them a good many times, till he could do them well, and she would give him another lesson when she came again. After this, she often looked in, and very kind she grew; and, like every body else, she told my wife all her troubles,—an odd thing to me; but I take it they looked upon her as a kind of nurse. Her father had been quite a gentleman, but spent all his money while he lived; and when he died, his house and all his land went to the eldest son. It seems unnatural, but I believe it's true; for I know when my lord died, my lady and all the children had to leave the park, and live in a small house some miles off, and their eldest son, a very wild fellow, came into all. Poor Miss Laura had to go out for a governess, and came into a family, not far from our squire's, to teach their daughters. The master was as nice kind a man as ever lived; but the lady hadn't been brought up with gentry, and nobody could bear her, she was so mean and unhandsome in every thing she did.

The night Miss Laura came to our cottage so wet she had been sent to a house a good bit off, to get her out of the way, because some young ladies were coming to the Grange; and visitors liked her company more than they did her betters'. She did not have a great deal of money given her, though she could talk a many strange languages; and has made us stare many a time to hear her sing to our children songs of people that live over the seas, and so natural, too, it seemed no trouble at all to her. But

it was not want of money she complained of
when she was talking free and easy to my
wife, but the being looked down upon, and
the way the servants treated her, copying
like after their mistress. My wife, who
knew a little about these things, when she
could do so and not give offence, used to
recommend her to wait on herself all she
could, and show a kind way to them; and
when she tried it, she said she found there
was nothing she couldn't do for herself, and
how much better she got on. We missed
her a great deal when we lived in the village; for when the children were ill, she
was forbid to come and see us, for fear of
carrying home the complaint; though it was
all an excuse, for it wasn't at all catching.
About two months before I went back to
the squire's, she went into his family, after
their governess married, and then we saw
her again, and times were better with her;
and to show she hadn't forgot my wife's
kindness in former days, she had made her
the present of the shawl and shoes; and,
unknown to us, had told the squire how
glad I should be to go back to my old place
again; and begged my master to take me

on as soon as ever she heard the other
gardener was going. Nobody seemed happier than she was when she came late in the
evening, and saw us all settled in comfortably again; and then she told us how it
was the gardener left. He was a very respectable young man, and came from a good
place; but he had married a fine-looking
young woman, who had been brought up to
the dressmaking. Her mother, like a foolish
woman, instead of teaching her how to clean
house, cook, and so on, and getting her into
a respectable family, said her daughter should
never be a slave, and gave her too much her
own way. Well, when she was married and
had two or three children, she made a poor
slovenly housekeeper, and was very untidy
in herself. On Sundays she made a good
show, but on week-days she was down at
heel, and her clothes hung about her as if
she had been dragged through the bushes;
and so you may guess how the garden-room
was kept. A good deal of fault was found
at its being so dirty and dusty; but she
wouldn't bear speaking to, and at last persuaded her husband to give up his place,
and take a bit of land near a neighbouring

town, and turn master for himself,—a kind
of market-gardener.

Poor Miss Laura! trouble did her and
all of us good; it was just like a heavy fall
of snow over the spring flowers, it kept us
in our right places; and when it melted
away, we never enjoyed the sunshine more.
She afterwards married very well, to a young
farmer; but she soon died, in childbed, and
lies in our village churchyard. He's gone
away over the seas, so I've heard say; but
wherever he is, he'll never forget her, nor
I either, the generous young lady: I wish
there were more like her.

When she went away, the evening we
got back and I'm telling of, the foreman
came in, and I got my lantern, and we walked
round the houses together. There seemed a
good deal of alteration, and the plants looked
uncommonly well; but I laid it all to the
candle-light; but next morning I found
there was no mistake; the man that had
gone away was a deal cleverer than I was.
I could see that with half an eye. Every
thing was in the best of order, and so many
new plants. So, said I, it will not do to get
behindhand: and ever since I've took in all

the different gardening books and papers I
could afford, and more; and I often went
and looked at other places, and saw what
other people were doing. You may stop at
home and look at your own doings till you
think you cannot be beaten; but I've learnt
there's nothing like looking about you; and
however well you may do a thing, try and
do it better.

I did not see the squire for some time
after I got back, for the family went away
the next day; but when he came home, and
into the garden, I was nailing some trees,
and he came beside me before I was 'ware
of it, and looking very slily and kindly, he
said, " Is that you, Gregory?"

" Yes, sir," said I; "and very much
obliged to you I am for all favours."

" You will have nothing to thank me
for," said he, " if you do what I wish; and
if I tell you to cut off half the trees' heads
in the orchard, I'll have it done, though I'll
hear all you've got to say against it; and I'll
not blame you if I do wrong. If you gardeners don't take care, you'll sicken half the
masters in the country, and they'll employ
labourers instead; for I'd rather plough my

E

place up than have a man in my service that thinks himself too great to do what he's told and when he's told. If I want my land cropped to my fancy, do you think my bailiff is to do as he pleases? No; he's too much good sense for that; but half of you gardeners mustn't be interfered with; and that makes gentlemen care so little about changing a gardener."

He then walked away; but I soon heard his voice again, and I thought he spoke as if he was angry, and I'm sure my foreman was, for it was he the squire was talking to; but as I didn't see him before the men left work, I didn't hear what it was about just then.

In the evening, after tea, in comes the foreman into my cottage, looking as red as a turkey-cock, and as stupid as an owl in daylight, and the king's English had got so hard to him all of a hurry, that he couldn't get some of his words out. " I won't stand it, that I won't," he kept stammering out; " and you may tell him so to-night, when you go up to the house. I'm as good a man as he is, though he is so rich; but I don't care; no, that I don't. I do my work; and what business are my clothes to him? his money didn't pay for 'em; and if they are patched, that's no business of his. You tell him, I won't stop; no, that I won't. I don't care; no, that I don't;" and so he went on.

I saw in a minute what the squire had scolded him about; but I let him go on without saying any thing, for talking to a tipsy man is like putting dry leaves on a bonfire, —it only makes it blaze the more. "Come," says I, "just go with me, will you, and let's see if any of those boys are in the upper garden, stealing the potatoes out of the pits; you take that lantern, and I'll take my own;" and he grew so maudlin to me; and then he'd abuse the squire, and tell me to be sure and mind that he wouldn't stop, no, that he wouldn't, if he'd go down on his bended knees to him. When we'd got out of doors it was raining finely, which I knew well enough; and he asked me to lend him something to put over his shoulders. "Never mind a drop of rain," says I; "come on; you don't care for a little wet, do you?" I took him the worse road and the longest way, and it pouring hard all the time. He soon left off talking about not standing it;

and his voice got clearer, and he said such a
night as that no boys would be out stealing
taters. " We'd better be sure," said I; "and
you take the outside the garden-wall, and I'll
go in; and be sure you catch 'em if I halloo."

When I thought he was downright well
soaked, I called to him over the wall, and
said there was nobody about; and we'd go
home again, if he'd go back to the gate.
How he shivered and shook, to be sure, when
we met! he was as clear-spoken too as I
was; and when I asked him if he was wet,
then he said he was, for his clothes were old,
and he'd got some holes in them. " I suppose, then," said I, " the squire was telling
you of them holes." " Yes," said he, "and
angry enough he was." " Well," said I,
"you get home as quick as you can and
shift yourself; it's no use your going to my
cottage; the sooner you're dry the better;
so good night." " Good night," said he;
but perhaps you'd better not say any thing
to the squire to-night." " Ah, but," says
I, "suppose he says something to me, and
says you're to go." " That'll be a bad job,"
said he; "and perhaps you'll say a word
for me." " Well, good night," said I; " get

home as soon as you can, and I'll see you to-morrow."

I shifted myself when I got in, and then went up to the house ; and after I had given in my book, and got all settled, just as I expected, the squire began. " Gregory," said he, " that man David must be sent about his business—a ragged fellow ; surely he earns enough to keep decent clothes about him. I'm afraid he drinks too much ; there's a something about him I don't like,—he never looks comfortable,—and when I happen to drop upon him unawares, he always seems to wake up and move faster at what he's about ; and that's a thing I never like to see, for it tells plainly that he's only an eye-servant, and an eye-servant I will not have. I like a man to feel as much pleasure in earning his wages as I have in paying them. Come," said he, " Gregory, tell me how you account for it ; can he afford better clothes, or can he not ?" " I ask your pardon, sir," said I, " and mean no offence ; but if you'll let me tell you all I've thought about it, maybe I shall do no harm, and you'd be better pleased than if I held my tongue." " Go on," said he. " Well, sir," said I, " you see

he's all you say,—he's ragged and he drinks,
and he does no more work than he can help;
and all shows that he's got no respect for
himself, so 'tisn't likely he'll have much for
other people; if he had, he wouldn't have
spoke to you as he did.   He was a decent
lad when he first came; but I thought he
didn't get much better before I left, and I
used to tell him he went out too much of
nights.   Since I've been back, I went up
one evening to his room, to talk to him about
getting to the King's Head, and stopping
out so late.   He wouldn't say it was wrong;
but he said, ' Look here, who's to spend his
time always in this place ?   Look at the
walls, how damp they are.'   And so he went
on, finding fault with every thing.   I told
him the other two men had just the same
lodgings, and they found no fault.   ' Not to
you,' said he, ' but they say plenty to me.' "
The squire stopped me when I'd got so far,
and said, " I'll look to it; you meet me at
their rooms to-morrow at ten o'clock."

Next morning I was there, and showed
him how damp and wet the rooms were,—
too near the ground, and never a bit of sun
ever to shine in front of them.   " Now, sir,"

said I, "if I may be so bold as to say so much, I think if you'd be so good as to put up some rooms just over against the poor men's gardens, with the backs of them looking into the grounds, and the fronts to the south, that I could manage to make the men more respectable, or get some that would be; and if you'll make them a bit ornamental, I'll see that they shall be kept clean and tidy, and no dissight to the place. Bad rooms drive men to public-houses; for you'll see the difference in comfort, sir, if you look any evening into the tap-room of the King's Head, and then in here. 'Tis a wonderful temptation to a poor man, that a rich one knows nothing about; and a good many that blame him the most ought to say the least." He heard me very kindly, and then went to the place I wanted him to build on, and said he'd see to it, for he'd got many things to think of that he'd never thought of before; "And who knows," said he, "but David may be mended? and so do not discharge him, but tell him he's on his good behaviour."

Gardeners, like other working people, are often imposed on by a set of lazy begging fellows, who never did a day's work in a garden in their lives; and good care they take to know very little, or nothing at all, if they're questioned. Just to set others on their guard against these scamps, I'll have a say about one I met with that beat all I ever saw of the sort.

I happened to be giving him something to eat at my door, when the squire was coming by, and asked what he was; and when I said he was wanting work in a garden, and was badly off with walking about looking for a place, he told me to send him up to the house. As far as his clothes went, he was indeed badly off; for if it hadn't been for an old greatcoat to cover his rags, he'd have passed for a scarecrow. Well, the squire had him into an out-house, and had him stript, and gave him some decent clothes, and made quite another man of him; and the butler said he was so grateful, and spoke so pleasant, and told such tales of his hardships, and how it was every body's fault but his own that his misfortunes had come from, that they clubbed round in the servants' hall, and gave him six shillings to start with. The squire had a look at him before

he went, and put another half-crown to it;
though, as he said after, it was all from
what the butler had told him; but when
the butler was twitted about it, he said it
was all the girls' doing, because he looked
so taking after he was washed and dressed
up in the squire's old clothes; and they
persuaded him that he must be no impostor.

Well, the next morning the squire was
going to the town, as it was a bench-day,
and bid me take the light cart and go with
him, as he wanted to pick out a few things,
just to help on the gardener, that I've told
of before, that had turned nurseryman. He
rode on just before me; and about a mile
away from home, I saw him draw his horse
up to the bank-side all of a hurry. When I
came up, he said: "Gregory, isn't this the
man that was begging at our place yester-
day? He says he isn't." "Yes, sir," said
I; "there's no mistake about that." No
sooner had I said the words, than he raised
himself up—for he was lying down—and
says: "Well, what if I am?" "Why,
then," said the squire, "you're an impostor,
and an ungrateful rascal; and I'm a justice
of the peace, and I'll give you fourteen days

at Bridewell." "Do," says he, "and welcome; I've been in a good many times, and
never came out but I'd learnt some new
move or other. I've nothing to thank you
for," he went on; "you'd have spoilt my
trade altogether by dressing me up, only I'd
the luck to change your old clothes for
these; and we drank your health into the
bargain."

The fellow's impudence tickled the squire;
and when he saw he'd been drinking, and
was mighty talkative, he gets off his horse,
and bidding me hold his head, said to him:
"Come, you're a clever rascal; give me
your history, and I'll give you another half-
crown. Where do you come from, and how
do you live?" "With all my heart," says
he, "only let's have the half-crown down.
I don't come far from here—only the next
village : but I've been away so long nobody
knows me; and what brought me here I
can't tell now; though I did seem to think,
before I got here, that I must have a look
at the old place, and the fields. again where
I'd played : but now I wish I hadn't come.
I was made a beggar of from a boy, and that
no great fault of mine either. I was bird-

keeping on a bit of seeds, and had an old
gun and a little powder, and I thought I
might as well try and kill some as well as
frighten 'em; so I put some little gravel-
stones a-top of the powder, when, as luck 'd
have it, there came through the steward's
hedge one of his fowls. I up with my gun,
without a thought, and let fly. I was close
to him, and knocked him over; but the next
minute I was in the clutches of the gardener,
and hauled off to the constable; and from
the constable to the Bridewell for fourteen
days: but, after all, 'twas more to spite my
father than any thing else."

"No fault of yours, no doubt," said the
squire. "You must not interrupt me," says
the rogue, "or I can't tell my story." Says
I, "Why don't you get up, and treat the
squire as you ought to do?" for I felt quite
mad with the fellow's impudence. "Time
enough for me to do that," says he, "when
I'm brought afore him: you that pick his
bones may do it know." I thought at this
I should have fell upon him; but says the
squire, "Don't interrupt him, Gregory. Let
me hear what spite had to do with your
going to prison."

"Why," said he, "my father was what they call a jockey-man, and jobbed about with things,—hay and straw, and sometimes poultry, which my mother reared. He'd a good many pigeons, too, which the farmers sometimes complained about. One day the steward's two sons, who were home for a holiday, were going by with their guns, and none the more out of spirits for stopping a little while at an ale-house just by, when they let fly amongst the pigeons on our barn-top, for a wager who'd kill the most. My mother saw 'em, and they saw her; but they cut off like the wind, though not so fast but my father caught 'em; when they denied it altogether, and wouldn't pay; so he had 'em up, and then they had to pay the dearer; and this made the steward mighty angry. When I was caught, my father was away; but my mother went and offered to pay for the fowl, as they'd done for the pigeons; but the justices wouldn't hear any thing she had to say about that, and so to Bridewell I was sent. Well, the same day a fellow was sent there for a vagrant, and he soon showed me how to get a living without bird-keeping; and instead

of going home when my time was up, I
went off with him; and I've seen something
since then, I can tell you: and 'tis just like
any other trade—you're always a-learning;
and that made me say I shouldn't care for a
fortnight in the stone jug. Another thing,"
said he, "look here;" and he pulled open
a hole in the ragged trousers he'd now
got on, and showed a great sore. "There,"
said he, "that's bad, but it's earnt me a
trifle; for when I act the sailor, I say how
I got it at sea falling off the mast when it
was struck with lightning; though, to tell
the truth, I got it dancing, when I was
about drunk, in a pot-house, and fell on a
labourer's pickaxe, that the fellow had put
right in the way of honest people. It's
rather too sore now," said he, "and a little
rest'll do it good; so if you'll let me ride in
the cart, you may commit me, if you like;
only don't make it for too long, nor put me
to hard labour."

Dear, how the squire did laugh at the
fellow's impudence! "*I* commit you!" says
he; "no, that I won't; why you'd spoil a
jail, and all in it. But you said I'd done
you harm by giving you better clothes; how

do you make that out?" "Easy enough," said he. "It's no matter how you're dressed when you beg of the poor, if you've only a good tongue, and fit your tale to the listener: but with people better off, you can't be too ragged; and if you can show a sore like mine, so much the better. The poor give because you get the better of their feelings, and they know what 'tis to want and to be hungry and a-cold; but the rich give you something because you make 'em feel uncomfortable, and they want to get you out of their sight."

"What do you say to that, Gregory?" said the squire. "Why, he's quite right," said I. "So he is," said my master; and he got on his horse, and off he rode: and I've learnt ever since then to give nothing away to people I know nothing about. I wrote all this down as soon as ever I got home, for I learnt more from that fellow than I'm likely to forget very soon. He said he'd never been to school; for his father used to say, "More school, more fool:" "But," said he, "if he had been able to write, like enough I might be able to find him; for then perhaps he'd have written to some one in the place, since he's moved nobody knows where."

As I was busy with the men one day making some alterations in the shrubberies, a gentleman, who lived not far off, came into the grounds, and walked on one side with the squire, and had a long talk with him; and then they beckoned me to them, when the gentleman said, " Gregory, what's your opinion of this case? My gardener is going to leave me, and claims a lot of plants, which he says he had given to him, and which are now some of the best in my conservatory. We're parting on very good terms, and I really wish to do what's right; but I don't mean him to take them away till I feel more sure than I do just now that he has any business at all with them. Now tell me honestly what you think about it as a brother-gardener; mind, I know nothing about them, whether he got them in exchange or not, but I've seen them in my house for more than a year."

I thought over it a bit, and then said, " I think I can get you an answer, if you'll go with me to our two old woodmen, and they're not far off; and I'd rather do that than give you one myself."

They were two old pensioners of the squire's,—two brothers that had worked in the plantations in his father's time from boys,—and the squire had let them have a little bit of ground on the sunny side of one of the spinneys; and there, under a couple of ash-trees, they'd built a bit of an arbour on the bank, where they used to sit every fine day, after they'd hobbled about awhile on their two sticks a-piece, and remind one another of what they'd done in their day, and what fine woods their work had grown into; and then they'd chuckle, and say, "Ah, there'll be no more such seen," and so on.

Well, the squire and his friend said they'd go; but I asked them to get quietly through the spinney just to the back of their arbour, and listen to them from there; for 'tis the hardest thing in life to get a poor man to speak what he thinks before what he calls his betters: they always answer just as they think they're wanted to do. When I got up to them, I bid them a good morning, and said, "Well, here you are, sunning yourselves again this fine autumn day;—talking about your woods, I suppose." "You may say that," said Ben, "for they are something to talk about; and neither you nor the squire, clever as you think yourselves, will ever make as good, going on as you do now planting so thin, and always hecking about in the young plantations as you do, for all the world as if you was hoeing turnips." I saw I should soon lose my hare if I let them hunt theirs, so I came to the point at once by asking whose trees they called them that they were sitting under. "Why ours, to be sure," said Ben; "didn't we plant 'em a pretty many years ago, when they was no bigger than this here stick of mine? and haven't we looked after 'em ever since, till they are as they are?" "Well," said I, "they're worth a trifle now to the wheelwright; why don't you turn 'em into money? they'd buy you some victuals, and warm clothes for your old bones." "Why there you are again, always a-jóking, Master Gregory," said Ben. "Tho' we call 'em ours, you know well enough they're the squire's; for tho' we got the saplings and planted 'em, 'tis the squire's land they grow on; and 'twas in the old gentleman's time, too, we used to fence 'em off, and so on, just when they wanted a little looking after, up to the day he christened 'em the Two Brothers, and they grew out of harm's way, and could take care of themselves. And I'll tell you what, Master Gregory, when we're both dead and gone, mind you say a kind word for keeping 'em up, or we'll pop out of our graves and haunt you."

"No, they shall never be cut down, Ben," said the squire, laughing, as he jumped out of the spinney with his friend after him; "I promise you that; and this gentleman and Gregory shall be witnesses that I'll charge your young master never to put an axe to them, but let them live in the sun and the wind, as you do yourselves, as long as they can." But, dear me, the old men hadn't another word to say, only in the way of thanking the squire and his friend, who put a shilling a-piece into their hands for what he called the best and cheapest counsel's opinion he had ever had.

A few days afterwards, the gentleman's gardener came to me, and said I had better mind my own business, and not interfere with other people's; and it was time enough for me to speak when I was asked, and a deal more of the same kind he threw out at me. I was sorry to see him so hot and angered; for he was a good kind of man, and we had been very friendly as neighbours; but he would not hear a word I had to say at that time.

However, I was not going to lose an acquaintance I respected that way; so I walked up and saw him in the evening, and told him just what I've put down here; and in a little while he saw with me that if a gardener grows plants at his master's expense of time and means, they must be left behind when he goes away, unless it is agreed between them that he may take them with him. I know his was a hard case, and so it is many a stirring man's that wants to keep pace with the times, when he buys or has given to him a few good things for himself, and makes his employer's place gay, to get no other encouragement than to be told to do as much that way as he can, and after all to have to leave them behind him. I've had this thing over many a time, and have heard men say that there shouldn't be a plant in a place unless the owner would buy them; but I can say for myself, and many others, that if a man loves his business, and wants to fit himself for some bet-

ter situation, if the chance offers, he must
do the best he can to get his hand in; and
every young gardener will find 'tis not throwing time and pains away to do so. The
squire always gave me full leave to give
away or exchange any thing we had to
spare; but he never would allow me to give
to people that could afford to buy, and yet
would rather beg. In his merry way, he
would say to such people, " There's so and
so the nurseryman, or the florist; I want to
see them thrive, and it's a real kindness to
give them a turn. Tell them I sent you,
and that the next time I see them I shall
inquire how they served you." He dearly
loved giving a striving man a helping hand,
happen how it would. One day, walking
up a hill, he saw a fellow with a donkey-
cart. Poor little Neddy was sadly over-
loaded; so what does the squire do, but get
behind and push till the cart was fairly at
the top, when squire, man, and donkey all
stopped to get wind. " You overload your
donkey, my friend," said the squire; "and
it's very cruel to the poor brute." " Ah,
master," said the fellow, " a good many
people's told me that; but you're the fust

as has ever pushed behind;" which was something like saying, " it's a deal easier to preach than to push."

What a blessing to a parish is a good clergyman! When I first came to Birdwood the rector lived there; but though he was a very good kind of man in his way, he thought so much of himself, and preached so learned, that poor folks could not understand it,—some would be asleep, and some would sit with their mouths as wide open as if he'd been shelling out sugar-plums, and they waiting to catch them. He'd come of a great family, and never knew much about the poor. But he changed away afterwards to somewhere else, as I heard; and the new rector brought with him for curate a middle-aged gentleman, and things soon took a turn, for he was always amongst us; and the people soon left off going to the dissenters' meeting, till there was hardly a dozen left, and they not the good, old, respectable folks, but of that comfortable kind that think some's born to be lost eternally, and some saved. Of course they themselves are all of the last sort, and very thankful I've heard them make themselves at the others' expense; as if God, that shows His goodness in all things in nature, shouldn't be good and just to all mankind alike. I hope to meet them in heaven, if it's only to see the conceit took out of 'em; for nothing but death will do it.

The rector didn't live in the village, but came always twice a year; but we heard say that he paid a great deal of the tithes to the curate, and well he deserved it. I'll just show the kind of man he was. One night, pretty late, he tapped at my door (for he never opened the poorest man's door without a rap), and when he'd sat down, he said, " Gregory, I've been speaking to Whittaker, your brother-gardener at the Grange, about your decorating the church together, with holly, against Christmas-day; but he tells me you're not friends now, and he'd rather do it alone." "Well," said I, "and he may, for I don't care if I never speak to him again as long as I live." " I'm sorry to hear that of two of my parishioners," said he; "but as I'm late, perhaps you'll be so good as to light me home into the village?" " With all my heart," said I, and got my lantern. As we walked along, he talked to me about loving my neighbour, and as life was uncer-

tain, that we couldn't live too well prepared
in every way for death; and he talked so
kindly, that though I was as determined as
ever not to speak to the man again, the time
seemed scarcely any before we got to his
door; and I was for saying good night, only
he asked me just to light him along his passage into the kitchen, which I was glad to
do. I noticed, when he shut the door after
me, that he locked it, and put the key in his
pocket; and it seemed odd, but I saw the
reason in a minute when we got into the
kitchen, for there stood Whittaker. "Now,"
said he, " I've got you here to ask you to
help me to a good night's rest, by knowing
you are friends again ;" and he repeated to
us both a deal he'd been saying on the way.
" Well," said I, "if Whittaker will beg my
pardon, I'll forgive and forget." " I've nothing to beg your pardon for," said he;
" what have I said or done ?" " Why," said
I, " you told the carrier, when I left Birdwood, that there was *some good reason* for
it, or I shouldn't have lost my place there ;
and you might as well have told the barber,
for I heard of it again, and more than once,
and it did me a deal of harm that I never

deserved." "I won't deny saying so," said he; "but I never meant to hurt you." "Come," said our minister, "shake hands, shake hands, and be friends again. When you've a parcel of rubbish in your gardens, neither fit for dung or to burn, what do you do with it, eh, Gregory?" "Why, bury it," said I; and we both laughed and shook hands, for there was no helping it; for the quarrel was just like the blacksmith's forge—you pull the handle, and it blazes up, and the more you pull, the fiercer it burns; but only let the handle alone, and it's soon out. "Now," said the minister, "I know I shall have a handsome church." And when Christmas-day came, our rector preached; and he told the curate after, it did his heart good to see such a church full of honest-looking, hard-working people and their wives, and to see all the seats and windows look so seasonable with holly and evergreens.

There was a gardener came into our village one spring, and it was nothing uncommon he came about; for it was only to be married to a young woman that belonged to our parts, and had been a fellow-servant of his. I can't quite see what makes all the difference, but I've noticed, in more people than gardeners, that when they've been about London they give themselves· a deal of airs amongst us country-folks, and try to make us believe that they're something more than we value 'em at; they'd have us think we know less than they do, and they expect us to believe it too. But we're rather unwilling to do more than listen; we do that as well as we can, though it's rather trying to one's patience.

One day I'd just got up from dinner, when the one I'm telling of came up, and asked if he might have a look round. I, thought what kind of a man I'd got hold of; so I first took him into the old garden and into the old houses—the ones I found when I came to Birdwood, and which we used just to keep bedding-out things and the orange-trees in, and some late vines overhead. These old-fashioned houses, with steep roofs, heavy sashes, small glass, and brick flues, soon set his tongue loose, and he began to talk very large about *my* place and *my* plants, *my* houses, and *my* every thing. He used such fine words, too, that I could not tell what he meant; and he pulled first one

thing and then another about, and, looking
at the orange-trees, which wanted new tubs,
said he, " These are doing badly; let me recommend you to get a little more *karbonic
hacid* gas into your soil, and you'll find it
wonderfully *venerate* 'em." " Well," said I,
" I have heard as much; but 'tisn't easy to
get it in a country place like this; perhaps
you'll be so good as to send me a little parcel down by the wagon from London that
passes by;" and I pulled out half-a-crown.
But he said he was sure it would not be
more than a shilling, and he would not forget it. He was going, till I said, "This
way," and took him through a door into the
new houses, a large range all heated with
hot water: one for stove and greenhouse
plants, one a fine grape-house, with divisions
for succession crops, and another with peaches
and figs; then, again, pits for cucumbers and
melons, and one for mushrooms. Though I
say it myself, they were a credit to us, if
nothing to boast of; and he thought so too,
for his eye caught mine, and there was something in it that stopped his tongue; and
when I began to ask him a few questions
how he did this and did that, he was all

over confused, and made an excuse to be off;
and I was glad to get rid of him, though I
didn't let him go without bidding him not
forget the *karbonic hacid* gas to *venerate* my
plants with. How foolish we are to use
words we don't know the meaning of!

But I must say a word about a very different kind of man—I'm afraid to say gardener; for if he's a standard for gardeners,
I'm not one, I'm only a labourer; and I'd
rather, if I had to start afresh, be like him
than be the greatest man in the land. He
was none of that wishy-washy sort that you
may wring like a dish-clout and get nothing
out of, but of that kind that says little, and
yet knows and can do much. How I wished
he'd lived only some few miles off instead of
in another county. I carried him a note
from the squire, who was a friend of his
lady's; and as I got to the place rather late
in the evening, I thought I'd walk to his
house and give him the letter, just to see
what kind of a greeting I was to get, and so
be ready for the morning. His little maid
took in the note, which brought him to the
door directly; and he had me in at once,
more like an old friend than a stranger.

The first thing he asked me was where I was going to sleep. I told him I'd got a bed at a publichouse near the park gate. "You don't sleep there," said he, with a merry smile; "that is, if you can bend your knees a bit, for my spare bed's none of the longest. And come," said he, "you must want something to eat and drink. I'm just going to tea, and I've a bit of cold meat and a keg of home-brewed in the cellar; so you shall not want."

"A cup of tea and a clear head, if you please," said I; "and with all my heart I'll make myself as welcome here as you shall be in my cottage at Birdwood, if you will but come and see me there."

While the women-folks were getting the tea, he took me into his room, where he was busy when I came to the door. He was looking through his multiplying-glasses at a little insect he'd found among some seeds just come over sea. He was drawing it; "But," said he, "I'll clear all this away, and we'll sit and have a chat; and I'll send for your things, and tell them at the public-house you're going to sleep here." I thanked him, but begged him not to clear the table, but to let me see any thing and every thing.

"Well," said he, "these are some seeds my lady's son, who is in Australia with his regiment, has sent me home. As soon as I opened them, I saw there was mischief among them; so, you see, I put my little magnifying-glass, which I always carry hung round my neck, to my eye, and I soon found the cause; and now you look through that powerful glass at your elbow, and turn that screw till you see something quite plain, and tell me what it is."

"Why," said I, "'tis like a crab, and all alive too." "Well," said he, "there's my drawing of it. Now those seeds have come 15,000 miles in a ship, but whether my friend was born on the voyage I cannot tell; but there he is, and that dust you see among the seeds is the chips he has made. But come, tea's ready by this time; and we'll not go out of doors afterwards, but we'll make a long evening of it."

So we went into the next room, and there was his wife with the tea all before her; and she, too, gave me such a welcome, that I felt easy in my chair directly. There

was a little in her tongue that sounded like
coming from Scotland, and it was a pleasure
to see and hear her; for her simple kind
face told what a good and gentle heart was
shining in it. She was dressed, too, as
plain and neat as my own good wife, and
the last person she seemed to think of was
herself; all was about others, and wishing
to see that we did well at what was set before us. Said I to myself, "You've got the
right kind of partner here, my friend." A
lad, too, came in out of the garden and sat
down with us. He had very little to say,
but I could see 'twasn't because he hadn't it
in him. After a hearty tea, for I was sharp
set, my friend went back to his little room,
and told his wife to show me their house
while he was busy for a few minutes.

I thought mine was a nice cottage at
Birdwood, and so it was; but this was most
capital : a living-room, a best room, his own
little room, a kitchen and scullery on the
ground-floor, three bed-rooms, and a kind
of cupboard-room above, and down below
a good large cellar. It was in the park,
at the gardens' entrance-gate, and had two
small greenhouses close to it.

By the time we'd gone over it he was ready for me, and had me into an arm-chair at his table; and, dear me, what a deal he showed me! There was a plan for alteration in the pleasure-gardens that was to be made: it was all drawn out and coloured for his lady to approve of; then there was a lot of drawings of fountains and vases for her to choose from, and rustic seats, arbours, and flower-baskets. Then he showed me a book full of painted apples and pears and other fruits, all to size of nature, as they had been gathered from the standards, espaliers, and off the walls, showing their differences. Then he pulled out a fruit-book, in which he put down every year the quantities of all kinds gathered season after season, with his notes about their keeping. He had got wax specimens of potatoes grown in their ground, modelled exactly, shape and eyes, the pink kinds coloured to nature. He showed me, too, dried plants, and wonderful drawings of every kind of fern, all neatly put in books; and, indeed, made me wish, for the first time in my life, that I was a young man again, I felt so ignorant, and saw so much to learn. I was at home with most of the fruits and

potatoes, but nowhere else; and he surprised
me with his drawings of his seedling grapes,
his currants and gooseberries, his every thing,
indeed; and he had all particulars about
weight, size, and quality, what was kept,
and what was done away with. Then he
had little samples of glass, of tiles, of sashes,
of boilers, of cocks and valves; indeed, of
almost every thing he could want about the
gardens. And while he showed me all these,
he was so modest, and seemed so pleased to
explain to me every thing I wanted to know.
He saw how much I enjoyed it, and that I
made no pretences to be what I was not, but
that I was only a practical man.

We did not get to bed till near midnight,
after a bit of supper; and then he put me
into a nice room, so well furnished, with all
the walls hung round with his own drawings
of many things; and instead of a little bed
a fine large one, and all beautifully white
and clean; with plenty of little pretty orna-
ments on the mantle-shelf, and a Bible and
Prayer-book on the dressing-table: just as
much as to say, There's the food, take or
leave it, as you please; we've provided it for
those that'll relish it. As he bid me good

night, he asked me if I shaved myself, "For
there's no barber hereabouts," said he; "but
I can mow a chin on a pinch as well as a
lawn." "No, thank you," said I; "no man
ever took me by the nose yet, and I must
not let you do so, I'm sure."

I begged him to call me when he went
out at six in the morning; but I was up and
dressed all ready long before that, and looking out of the window on one large walled-in
square of kitchen-garden: beautiful standards
here and there, espaliers at the path-sides,
and handsome trees trained on the walls.
The two greenhouses I could see, one under
each window, but only could tell they were full
of colour. I opened the door as I heard his
footstep, while the garden-bell was ringing,
and had a kind hearty "Good morning;" and
down we went, and saw all the gardeners
and labourers come in,—and a very respect-
able-looking tidy lot they were; and as they
passed us at his door, all said, "Good morning," which looked so pleasant. He gave
them his different orders as they passed, and
then he took me all round. It's no use
making many words about it, every thing
was first-rate; from the mould-yard to my

lady's conservatory, there was not a spot from one end to the other that had a sloven's corner in it. Ice-house, fruit-room, potatoe and root store, every thing alike. Every tool was numbered, and had to be returned to its place; or the man that didn't do so was fined. I was a week there, and I never spent a happier one. My new friend was so kind, and wished me to see every thing, and was never tired of answering my questions; and there never surely was a merrier man, though he was a thoughtful one too, at times. The first morning, before breakfast, he asked me if I was ashamed to hear prayers read; and I said, "No, not a bit of it;" so in came the little maid, and he read part of a chapter; then we kneeled down, and he read a prayer, asking God's blessing, for Christ's sake, upon us and all dear to us, finishing with the Lord's Prayer. It was like oiling the wheels for a day's journey; and what a blessing, thought I, is such an example to these two young people! One of the mornings, when my friend had to go from home early, his wife took his place, and did the duty just the same. I sha'n't soon forget her voice and manner.

Two of the evenings we had some music and singing—pretty much Scotch, and here I was at home; and how the time did fly, to be sure! The last evening before I came away, a friend of theirs came in, and we finished off with "Auld Lang Syne;" and happy enough we were, tho' our "cup o' kindness" was but a cup of tea; but then 'twas sweetened with the heartiest kindness, as we took each other's hands all round, and finished off for a farewell. We wanted no stronger drink, and wished poor Burns had loved no other. I know something of the mischief drinking-songs do young people; it's just dressing up a skeleton. Part of the time I was with them, I wasn't very well, and then I stopped indoors, and so had time to see more of my friend's wife. They'd been married four or five years, and had no family; and as she was very clever in many ways, she was every thing to him. She helped him in his writing and drawing and making his models, and seemed quite to live for him, and in him; and shared all his love of gardening, which was wonderful, and made him a deal sought after by people that wanted help in such matters. He'd chuckle sometimes over what he read in gardening papers and books; and he once showed me a paper, too learned for me to understand, where a man thought he'd made a wonderful discovery, and other people thought so too, and he got more than praise for it; but my friend after a while upset the whole thing, though he thought nothing more of himself for doing it, but was pleased that he'd saved gardening a deal of mischief. He was so honest, too; for when the youngster that lived with them talked of the writer, and called him a humbug, my friend stopped him, and said he must not say so. The author had been too quick, and hadn't searched long enough, and been short of patience; and he bid the boy learn a lesson from it, and not make a guess and then try to prop it up, but go on thinking he might be wrong till he proved himself right. "Besides which," said he, laughing, "you ought to speak well of him; for if he hadn't made his blunder, I shouldn't have won my credit." It seemed this lad's parents wanted to make him a first-rate gardener, which was what he wanted himself, and so they sent him off several hundred miles from home to learn

his business at this place. He'd come of a
good stock, but it seemed to my friend and
his wife that it was running a great risk to
have him lodge in the town, and pick up
with one and another acquaintance; and so,
though they were so happy together, rather
than see him do badly, or run a risk of it,
they'd made a home for him with them for
a while, till he'd seen more, and been shown
a little of what's what. Now what could be
kinder than that? and it may be, and I hope
it will be, that some day he'll make such a
man as shall repay their goodness by being
what they'd like to see him; and perhaps
he may do some such kind thing for somebody else, as a token of his not forgetting
what he owes them. While I was there, my
friend gave a lecture to the mechanics in the
town, and to any body else that chose to go
and pay for a seat. His wife was obliged to
stop at home ; but how her heart was with
him, for he'd never been so public before. I
went; but said I to her, " Now don't you fret.
It's to be only an hour, and I'll sit near the ·
door, and directly it's over I'll run off, and
tell you all about how he's got through." It
was a great meeting, and a good many big-

wigs there too ; but every body listened as
if they begrudged losing a word: and all the
while he was speaking he was so simple and
so forgetful of himself, that I could but think
he'd have made a bishop.   At his last word,
as the clapping began, I cut off ; and when I
got near the house, I saw the wife's head at
the window, and open came the gate.   " All
right," said I, "go in ; I'll tell you all about
it ;" and wasn't she pleased ?   But she'd to
hear a deal more ; for, after I left, so many
stopped to tell him what they thought of his
success, that he was kept away a good bit
from getting home again to tell her all he
thought and felt.

Before I left, I sent a message in to his
lady to say that I was going home, and to
ask if there was any commands for the
squire, or any thing she wished to send
that way.   I was had into her room, and
she kindly asked me how I had liked my
visit.   I told her honestly what I thought of
every thing I had seen, and how happy I had
been.   " Well," said she, " I am glad of it.
They are excellent people, and if I had no
more trouble about my place than they bring,
I should have none at all; and it is all due to

good principles;" and then, giving me a few little books, she bade me give her best respects to the squire; and I took my leave of her, and soon after of my kind friends. He shook me heartily by the hand, and said he was glad I had paid 'em this visit; and she seconded all he had said. I'd nearly kissed her; for she had been so open and so kind, that I felt as if I was bidding good-bye to a daughter or a sister. I felt very dull as I left the gate; but when I was on the coach, the wheels wouldn't go round half fast enough, I wanted so much to get back to my Birdwood again. Hasn't England something to be proud of in such gardeners? and who can wonder at the place they take?

I've often noticed men can talk a deal better than they can think, and can measure out other people's corn, and give good measure, and sell it cheap too. If bread's dear, the farmer ought to be made to thresh out his ricks, and send to market all the wheat in his granary. If a man's poor, he ought to be kept, and well too, never mind how he got so,—the English of which is, that the careful ought to keep the spendthrifts. Then, again, what notions these kind of people have about having a fresh start, and sharing all things alike, and so on. Among these talkers, I once knew a shoemaker and tailor. They'd sit so long at the same stitch, stitch, that their thinking went in one rut too, and that always was, that if they weren't so well off as other people, it was every body's fault but their own; and to this they'd stick, nothing would turn them. These two always lost Monday, keeping away from their wives and homes, and going any where but where they should be, and minding every thing but their proper business. I once saw them basted with their own sauce, and it'll be long before they forget it, I warrant. A gentleman farmer, by bad management, had got under the drip, and had to be sold up root and branch. I had to go to the sale to buy a few things for the squire, and my brother-gardener and best friend, Mac Pherson, had to go too, to get a cow for his master. It was fine May weather, and we walked up to Knip Knolls, that we might look at the country and crops; and to my thinking there's no greater treat than a stroll thro' rich lands and good farming. Our walk made us peckish, and we went to a road-side

inn, hard by the place of sale, to get something to eat; and who should we first see,
amongst a lot more that were there only
losing their time, but this shoemaker and
tailor, out as usual, for it was a Monday.
We called for bread-and-cheese, and whilst
we were eating it they opened out their old
budget about the shame it was things were
so unequal : some so rich, and some so poor ;
some with so much land, and so many with
none ; and some such great folks that they
scorned the like of them, tho' the rich were
beholden to 'em for shoes and clothes ; and
wishing things was the same as in America,
where they was as they ought to be. What
the one said the other swore to ; above all,
they agreed that there ought to be in England a fresh start, and that no man ought to
have more of God's earth than another, and
nothing would be right till all was shared
out afresh. Mac and I had heard all this so
often that we didn't care to answer, but went
on with our bread-and-cheese, till they took
off, and ordered a rump-steak and onions;
and very particular they seemed about having it cooked with a bit of butter and dust
of pepper, for they were knowing fellows in

such matters, and proud of it too. By and by it was ready, and put on the table close by us ; but the tailor had gone to gossip with the people outside that had come to the sale, so the shoemaker went off to look after him, and in no good humour either. As soon as his back was turned, Mac whips off the cover, takes half the steak, divides it between him and me, and began eating away, whilst I could not think what he was at. Presently in they came, and seeing what we were doing, they began abusing us most unmercifully. I will say I felt very foolish, till Mac said to them, "What's the matter? did ye no say we ought all to begin again, and share and share alike ? We've only done what ye've been sae lang advising. Our bread-and-cheese was all gone, and we'd cum roun' to your way o' thinkin', and thought we'd make a beginning at once; so we've taken our share." But nothing of that kind of argument would suit them now, not a bit of it. They tried to hide how foolish they felt, but could not do it, tho' Mac went and ordered more, and paid for it, and as we went away said to them, "Dinna ding me ony mair wi' your clavers about starting afresh, and sharing and sharing all alike, ye gomeralls, ye. When it comes hame to yoursels, ye see clear eneugh what fools ye are ; and now take my advice, and wark o' Mondays like other folks, and drink less and chatter less, and ye'll hae mair for the wife and bairns."

I always liked a look at any thing that's going on, whether among gentle or simple. One day, when I went to the county-town, the landlord at the Crown and Sceptre told me there was to be a grand dinner at his house in honour of the Colonel, as they called him, for something he'd done in parish-matters in our parts. I knew the landlord very well, and asked him if he could give me a sight of it. " Yes, to be sure," said he, " if you'll stand at the side-board ; but your master's to be one of the party." " I don't mind that," said I ; " for I know if I ask him he'll not say no." So when he came into the inn-yard in his carriage, I spoke to him about it, and he gave me leave to stay ; " But," said he, "you'd better keep out of sight; for you'll make but a poor waiter, Gregory." It was the largest dinner-table I ever saw set out, and covered with silver and glass, a deal of which had been lent the

landlord, who was to have a guinea a-piece
for every ticket that was sold, whether people came or not. The company all got together in a large room, and chatted away till
the soup and fish were on table; when in
they came, and no trouble about seats, for
every gentleman's name was on a piece of
paper, and put on his plate. An old general, who lived just by, was in the chair,
with a lot of medals like crown-pieces on
his breast, which was padded out like a
pouter pigeon's, and told of the wars he'd
been in. The colonel—he'd been in the
militia—was on his right, and a clergyman
on his left, who, long before the noise of
seating the company was over, said grace;
but with so little in it like being thankful,
that I thought if it had been a charity-din-
ner, and the poor people hadn't said thank
ye better than that, it ought to have been
taken away again. The waiters knew their
business, and almost before people were in
their seats off came the covers; and there
was as pretty a buzz heard all over the room
as when a hive of bees think of swarming.
Eating and drinking's pretty much the same
with all sorts; and as the dinner went on,

it was fine fun to me to see how eager some were after the best cuts of the venison ; how they kept calling " Waiter !" so eagerly, all the while giving a glance at the joint as it was shrinking away ; and then, when they got a slice, how they turned it over, and looked pleased or sour, just as it was a good or poor one. Some seemed pretty much' lookers on, and our squire was one ; there he sat, as calm as a judge, hob-a-nobbing to one and another, letting the champagne go by, and always filling his glass out of a black bottle by him. But, dear me, every body liked him so much, and he had so many healths to drink at dinner, that I felt glad he had not to go home on horseback, but in his carriage ; for I thought he'd never keep sober, and so I told the landlord. " Never fear for him," says he ; " it's only toast-and-water he's got, though 'tis in a French bottle ;" and glad enough I was to hear it.

After the cloth was taken away, instead of grace after meat, three London singers got up and gave the company *Non nobis Domine*, in a way that pleased the company a deal more than it did God, I'll venture to

say, if I may guess from what I heard the
same men sing afterwards, when the bottle
had been pretty busy.   After the toasts
that's first given at all such dinners, the
old general gave a speech that wanted a
pair of crutches as much as he did himself,
—for he'd been a doer, not a speaker,—and
finished off with the colonel's health.   Then
he had to speak, but he couldn't make out
much better; but how the company did
cheer! for he was a wonderful favourite
with every body, and rich and poor all
said it was a pity he was so old.   The clat-
ter and noise wouldn't have stopped as soon
as it did, only after every toast there was a
song; and there was loud calls for silence
for the "Old English Gentleman."   When
that was finished, the noise was worse than
ever; and the landlord began to get all the
borrowed things off the table, changing
them for his own, for fear they'd be broken.
But what beat all in my eyes was when the
"Church and Constitution" was given.   I
could but ·think the Church had need of a
good constitution, if it was to stand such a
racket as was brought about it after it was
drunk.   The clergyman had to answer to

this; and, bless me, how he went on praising the colonel, as he looked at him as if he'd no more modesty than a monument, and had never a drop of blood to come up into his face in the way of a blush! I wondered the colonel did not get up and tell him he was but a poor simple bit of flesh and blood, and that he'd forgot himself, and wasn't in his pulpit praising his Maker; and so I said to the landlord. "But," says he, "let him alone; he knows what he's about; he knows the colonel likes it. We've all a weak spot in our noddles, and that's his; and, you see, some little time back, an old gentleman that had the living fall into his gift handed it over to the colonel, for him to give away as he liked, and he gave it to him that's speaking." As soon as the parson had done, the colonel rose again—just to say a word or two; but there was such a noise—such hurraing, stamping, and clapping—that it minded me of Herod; and glad I felt that I wasn't the colonel, for I should have been mightily afraid of being, like him, eaten of worms and dying; for I'm sure the company seemed as if they thought it the voice of a god, and not of a man.

After a while the better part left the
table, and went into another room for cof-
fee; but a many stopped to hear the London
singers, who seemed quite as ready to sing
dirty songs as the company that was left
was to listen and laugh and cheer. It was
late before the squire came away, and I
waited; for he'd told me to ride home behind the carriage, and send the boy back
with the light cart.

As I kept walking about the inn-yard,
waiting to go home, I saw the company
leave, and it set me thinking a good deal;
for I turned some of 'em in my mind into
poor men, and thought what a deal would
have been said about them and their noise,
and the money they'd been wasting in drink,
that ought to have been spent in better
ways. And like master, like man; for I
saw a pretty many servants that, if the
horses hadn't had more sense in their
brains than the drivers had got left in
theirs, more would have slept in the ditches
than in their beds that night. Our coachman said it didn't end there; for many a
poor horse, after rough riding or driving,
would have to put up with very little but

abuse and bad commons when they got home ; " For drink," said he, " is a very devil to poor horses and other animals, as well as to men." When I got inside my cottage, what a little heaven it seemed, after what I'd left behind and seen that night!

When I got into breakfast one morning, my wife said to me, " There's the constable been up looking for you ; for Andrews's in trouble, and he sent you a message to say that he hoped you'd go down and see him." " Give me a bit in my hand," said I, " and I'll go at once." But she persuaded me to get my breakfast ; " For," said she, " you'll have time to collect your thoughts a bit; and you never do any good being in such a hurry." Well, as soon as I'd done, I went into the village, and found the constable getting ready to take him before the magistrate. I asked him to leave me alone with him till he was ready to start ; but he took care to lock me in with him, which I told him he need not have done, for I'd be answerable for his not running away. " Mr. Gregory," said he, " I never trust myself ; so you may be sure I trust nobody else. 'Safe bind, safe find' 's my maxim ; and

H

if it's unpleasant to hear the key turn on you, and make you feel a prisoner, you'll find it like music to hear the bolts shoot back again when I let you out."

"Now, Andrews," said I, "what's all this about? When you worked under me, scold you as I might, I never had to say you told me a lie." "No," said he, "and I won't do so now. I've stole some of my master's coals, and there's no denying it; and all I want you to do is to come and say a word for me before the Bench; for I'm sure to be committed, and shall have to appear to-morrow." "Well," said I, "that I'll do; and it's no use our talking more now, for here's the constable coming; but I must have you tell me all about it, and I'll see you again this evening if I can, and if you're sent to the cage."

This Andrews was a man that had worked in our grounds partly, and partly at the house—a kind of odd hand—sometimes here and sometimes there; and he wasn't quite as nice as he should have been about little things, helping himself to fruit off the walls, or the like. I once had a good talk with him about it; and this was what brought it on. The squire ordered me to send to a family a little way off some grapes and wall-fruit, for a party they were going to have. I sent it by him in one of my boxes, and locked up, as I always did send it every where; for I can't bear to have my fruit dished up with all the bloom off it. And I sent the key in a letter to the footman, telling him how to put it on table, so as to be a credit to me; for nothing's so vexing to a gardener as to have it handled, as if it was all the better for being rubbed about like a parcel of oranges, which, without you tell 'em not, half the servants will do. I found I'd left out some nectarines by mistake; and so I looked Andrews up, to go back again, and I found him very busy over some cold fowl and a great piece of fine ham. " Where did you get that?" said I. "They gave it to me at Woodside," he said. "Well, Andrews," says I, "you know I'm no meddler in other people's matters; and if I say a word, and ask a question, you must take it in good part; for it's no use being offended. Did the mistress give it you, or the maid?" "Why," said he, "the cook did." "Then," said I, "you shouldn't have taken it, that

I know." "How can you know that?" said
he. "Come," said I, "a word will settle it.
How did you bring it away?—openly in
your hand, or how?" He was still a minute; then he said, "I may as well say at
once, you're right; for she bid me let nobody see it." I didn't know then that the
cook and he kept one another's company.
"Now, Andrews," said I, "I'll be as honest
with you. The old footman has often told
me that his mistress is one of the kindest
and best of women; but she will give every
thing away herself, and she says that none
of her servants have any more right to take
her victuals and give it away than she has
to go to their boxes and take their money or
clothes to give to the poor, or what not.
And she's quite right, too; and it's a pity
such kind people shouldn't have honest servants about them." I saw he was out of
temper about it, and couldn't account for
it till I heard afterwards that they were
sweethearts; but I kept on, and said I,
"Take care, Andrews; you know I've often
told you about taking my wall-fruit. It
seems a little thing, but you'll find it isn't:
'tis just like cutting a little bit of a gap in

the bank of our high pond; it will get bigger and bigger in ordinary times; but if the spring comes down a bit stronger after heavy rain, the bank would go down altogether. It will be so with you, if you don't take care; for some great temptation may come, and then look out." "No fear of that," said he. "Well," said I, "you'll go back again with the nectarines, and I don't care if you tell the cook what I say; and mind this, if ever you want a bit of fruit, ask me, and if it's right you shall be sure and have it; but don't you be so silly as to meddle and help yourself to any thing that doesn't belong to you. And if you'll take my advice, you'll never take any thing again of any house-servant without first knowing whether their masters or mistresses allow of it; for, I can tell you, it's not a bit better than stolen goods; and it's a pity people should be so foolish as to try and make themselves believe that there's no harm in taking other people's victuals, though they'd call it thieving if it was clothes, or any thing else."

In the evening, down I went again to the cage, and then Andrews told me all about the trouble he'd got into. " When I got the place down at the Canal Wharf," said he, " you know I married the cook at Woodside ; and if we'd been more careful, we might have done very well, for I'd good wages. But we went along too fast for working-people, though, from my wife's account, it was a strange coming-down to her, that had had the best of living in her place. But I don't blame her at all, for I might have seen it wouldn't be easy to leave such a way of living as she'd been used to. When she was put to bed and I had the doctor to pay, and things to buy for the child, I began to find it out ; and by the time we'd three children, we got back a good deal : and so you'd have said if you'd come our way and looked in, which I was glad you didn't ; for I've often thought of what you told me in bygone days. When it cost us more to live, I couldn't earn any more ; and little by little I began to take one thing and another,—sometimes a little bit of corn for our pig, or a bit of coal,—and at last master found me out taking some in a bag."

When he'd done, said I, " I don't see how I can help you ; for what can I say about a man that's robbed a good master that's paid him good wages?" "Well," said he, "that's partly true and partly not; for there's a pretty many tricks goes on at that canal side that'll make the honestest of men thieves for their masters, if not for theirselves—like giving short measure and light weight." "Come, Andrews," said I, "that won't do now; nobody will believe you if it's ever so true; you should have said that before you were caught, so you may as well hold your tongue about it; and take my advice, and when you're before the Bench say nothing, and then perhaps your master will say a word for you; and I'll go over, and, if I can, I'll say a word myself, if the squire won't object."

In the evening, one of Andrews' mates comes up to my cottage, and says, "If you'll not turn upon me, I'll tell you how to help him a bit out of the trouble. There's a ton of coals in our cart, and master's told us to make it easy for the horse, as he calls it, and he stood by all the time we loaded. The people they're for sent word to put off sending 'em for a day or two; and if you can

get somebody you know to order a load, and
only weigh 'em, you'll find our master out;
for he's a big fool to think he can serve a
man out that way for doing only a little for
himself what he makes us do every day for
him, when he thinks he won't be caught."
" Now," said I, " don't make a fool of me."
" Never fear," said he; " it's all right." The
jobbing man that bought cows and things for
the squire lived close by; and I went to him
and put him up to taking the order over,
and to make sure and get the load I'd told
him of; and so he did, for next morning in
came the coals. When the carter asked him
where he was to put 'em, " In my scales,"
says he, " first" (and he hooked up his calf-
scales), " and then up in that corner." The
carter was master's man all over, and tried to
get off this; but these dealing-chaps, what
with going to fairs and bargaining, why
there's nobody a match for them with the
tongue; and so weigh 'em he must, and
there was pretty well two cwt. short. " I'll
fetch the rest up," says the carter. " Very
well," says the dealer; and when he'd shut
the gates, he said to me, who was waiting
out of sight, " *We'll fetch him up;* and now

you jump in my cart, and I'll drive you over to the Bench."

After Andrews' master had laid his complaint against him, and just as he was asked what he had to say for himself, up jumps the dealer, and says, " I beg your worship's pardon for being so bold, but maybe you'd not sentence him till I've said a word." " To be sure not," said the chairman; " if you're a witness, let us hear what you have to say; but he said he had no witnesses." " Why," says the dealer, edging up alongside the prisoner, "I don't know that I've much to say for him ; but I want to lay a complaint against his master for selling short weight, and so robbing people and making his servants thieves." "Stand down," said his worship; " that has nothing to do with this case ;" and then there was a bit of whispering among the magistrates, and laying their heads together, and then the chairman told the constable to take Andrews down, for sentence was put off a little. There was no other case, and then the dealer had his say, and told all about the coals he had had in, and how short weight they were ; and he wanted the justices to tell him what he was to do in this matter. All the while he was speaking, Andrews' master kept changing colour like a maid at a marriage; and when he was told to explain the thing, he went on finely against the dealer, and asked if they'd take the word of a man that lived by taking people in with lame horses and sick cows, and never told the truth only by mistake. But that wouldn't do for the justices, and so they granted a warrant against Andrews' master to appear next bench-day; but not before he'd said that he didn't want to be hard upon Andrews, who was sent to gaol for a month. Next bench-day his master had to pay a fine; but where's the justice of that, I should like to know? Why shouldn't master have gone to gaol as well as man? They were both thieves, and of the pair the master was the worst; and it's my belief, too, that half the men that's found out, like Andrews, either learn roguery of their masters, or, if they're bad, are made worse by them.

If there's one place where gardeners and their masters, and amateurs, show off worse than another, it's at a flower-show. When we first got up a society in our parts, it was

only among a few little people; and it was
only for such things as Polyanthuses, Au-
riculas, Pinks, Carnations, Picotees, and Pan-
sies. Well, the job was to find judges; and
when we got 'em, they pleased nobody but
those who had the prizes: *they* said how
lucky we were to get such clever men; the
others said there wasn't a judge amongst
'em. And then to hear the talk when we
got over our pipes and pots after the show;
and to see the sly old landlord, who was one
that showed too,—how he'd come in when
we'd got settled down a bit, and set us by
the ears about our pips and pastes and
lacings, and full flowers and thin ones—the
old fox, he knew well enough the pot never
empties so fast as when the tongue gets
dry with arguing. Dear me, I've known a
pretty deal of his small beer turned into
strong at such times, doing what he called
double duty—

> Sobering the brains,
> And helping his gains.

But after a while the gentry got up a society,
which swamped the little ones like ours with
its two-and-sixpenny prizes. But, with all the
talk, it was pitiful work; for there was just

as much jealousy among our betters as among
us, that wanted a better example. One that
lost wouldn't let his gardener show again;
and another found fault because his man
wasn't put first, instead of last; and then
the prizes, such as they were, not being paid
till next year, and one thing and another,
made my master and me only lookers-on. I
must say one thing, that the gardeners and
little people made things worse than they
might have been; for they'd fall so by the
ears in the room when the company came in,
and some of 'em smelt so of drink, that a good
many kept away that would have paid to
have come in and seen the flowers and vege-
tables. We might have had a fine show, if
our gentry would have followed our squire
as he would have led. He wanted them to
subscribe tens of pounds a-piece, and raise a
handsome sum, and put it to interest, and so
have some prize-money always in hand; and,
by way of example, he offered a hundred
pounds to begin with; but nobody would
follow, though they'd spend twice as much
on the subscription pack of hounds, or a
ball. But, talking of shows and gardening,
there's no place like London and thereabouts

for both; and before I'd lose such a sight, if
I was a young man, I'd walk every foot of
the way, that I would!

When I went up to London, the squire
got me an order, so that I might go to Chis-
wick early on the show-day, and see the
plants put up in their places; and I never
could have believed any body that had told
me all I saw with my eyes that day.   I
seemed lost in a wood of plants, as I walked
about in the tents, where the gardeners put
them down before they began to stage them:
—and such a set of men, too; why, their
helpers were better dressed and better man-
nered than the head men in our parts; and
yet, when I asked a question now and then
of some of 'em, they didn't seem to want for
conceit.   As good luck would have it, I met
a gardener that lived once not far from Birdwood, and had left to go into a London nur-
sery.   I should not have known him, but he
made me out; and very kind he was.   After
all the plants were staged, and it wasn't
till just before ten,—and I'd got to Turnham
Green by six,—my friend said, " I wish I
could get you a ticket for breakfast; but I
have got so little here, I know Doctor Lind-

ley won't give me one for you." "Oh," said
I, "I'll ask him myself." "You'd better
not," said he; "for you'll get no ticket, and
like enough something from him that'll serve
you instead of a breakfast." Says I, "There's
not a man's face on earth that I'm afraid of.
I've often heard of the Doctor, and read a deal
more; and now I'll have a look and a word
for myself, if you'll just show him to me."
"Come along," says he, and away we went.
After a longish hunt, he showed me a gentleman sitting on a stool under a tree, with a
walking-stick in his hand, and a pair of spectacles on his nose; and said he, "That's the
Doctor." "Thank you," said I; "and now
wait a minute for me." So I went up, and
lifted my hat, breaking ground, as my poor
father, when he was soldiering, would have
called it. "Well," said he, "what do you
want?" "I should thank you, sir," said I,
· "for a breakfast-ticket, for I'm a stranger,
and a long way from home." "What have
you brought, gardener?" "Nothing, sir,"
said I, "but myself; but I have sent something," said I, "before to-day; but not to
these shows:" and I showed him a silver
medal I had had sent me, through my mas-

ter, for a basket of fruit. "These break-fast-tickets," said he, "are for exhibitors and helpers only ; but I will give you one : and there," said he, handing me another, " that will admit you after one o'clock; for it is not often I see so much of the country as you have brought with you." He looked me all over,—at my knee corduroys, my leather gaiters, and at my canary waistcoat and long blue coat with metal buttons, and then into my face, as if he'd have burnt a hole in it,—all the while asking me questions, and wetting his fingers at his lips, and then running them over the cards in his hand. As soon as he stopped, I lifted my hat, thanked him, and bid him good morning ; but not before I'd heard him refuse tickets to two gardeners running — one because his plants were not all in their places, or all to rights, and to the other because he was so dirty and untidy. As they walked away by my side, they did abuse him, I tell you ; talking loud on purpose for me to hear. But my friend soon came to me ; and how he did chuckle at my good luck, as he called it ! " Well," said I, "you see none of us are so bad as we're sometimes made out; and now what I've thought all along I'm sure's right. If he's been down on the gardeners, like he was on the two you saw with me coming away from him, there's been faults on both sides, depend on it." "You're right there, Gregory," said he, "and that's the truth; and you never saw people so improved in your life as we gardeners are; and so you'll say when we get to the breakfast-room. Come along." I said it to their faces, and I'll say it behind their backs, that I wouldn't have believed there was such a set of gardeners as I saw there that day, and the young ones in particular. They'd have been none the worse for a little less of Jack Brag, and a little less talk about "my governor," and "my old man," and "my old lady," when they spoke about their employers; for I like to see a man speak with respect of those he serves. They rubbed me a pretty deal when we got free and easy after breakfast; but my friend said there was always a deal of "chaff" at such times and in such talk; and I quite believed him from what I heard. But, dear me, what a breakfast we had, and what a pleasant sight to see such care taken for gardeners! and then to see them when the company came, how different they behaved to what our country sort do! Why, they walked about amongst the gentry; and I never so much as saw any body look at any of them, as much as to say, Keep farther off, you gardener.

There was no stopping before the plants, and arguing, and all that kind of thing we see in the country; and I laid a pretty deal of it to the Doctor's treading so hard on their toes, and so making 'em keep moving. My friend said he thought it might be so, though he needn't have showed them up so hard; and they'd never forgive him for it, and calling them "practicals." "That's silly enough, too," said I, "after the medicine's cured you, to take offence at the doctor."

What with the flowers, and the company, and the music, and the place, I never was so glad as when I got back to London.

A few days after, I went to the show at the Regent's Park, and very grand it was, and the gardens wonderfully fine for such a smoky spot. When I had seen all I could of the plants, before the tents got crowded, I took a seat, and watched my fellow-crea-

I

tures, and that's no small amusement; and I saw a pretty many gardeners, too, enjoying the sight. Indeed, who could but look at those who came dressed out on purpose to be looked at. If looking at 'em pleased 'em, it would be selfish not to do it, especially when they couldn't learn your thoughts; and so you couldn't hurt their feelings, think what you would. To admire costs you nothing, and perhaps it gratified them, just as I once saw a young gentleman act on the top of a coach near London. It was stopping to take up, when a young blade rode by on a horse, sitting in his saddle just in a way that seemed to say, "Look here, every body." The young chap I speak of caught his eye, and bowed, and lifted his hat off his head to him. The horseman gave the bow back. "Do you know that fellow?" his friend that was beside him said. "Oh, no," said he; "but I thought it would please him, and it cost me nothing." So one man had his vanity tickled, and half-a-dozen of us that saw and heard were made mighty merry at nobody's expense; for the young blade neither saw or heard our merriment, and so rode on, well pleased at the notice he'd got.

CONCLUSION.

YOUNG gardeners, think of this: the man we've all come from, he was a gardener; therefore we've a right to say that ours is a noble business, for 'twas the first ever followed. He was set to gardening for pleasure; but he made a grand mistake, lost his place, and had afterwards to work for his living. He laid all his misfortunes to his wife, and that added to his disgrace; and it's my belief, from what I've learnt of a good wife, she would not have tried to get out of trouble, as he did, by saying, " My husband's to blame," if he'd committed the first fault. However, if she made the breach, through her came He who has repaired it; and when we think of this, we may all work on, and ought to find pleasure in our labour. If the thorns and thistles will grow, yet we are well repaid for the sweat of our brow by keeping 'em down; just the same as 'tis in our hearts: all kinds of evil things spring up there, every

body knows that ; but our business is to keep
hard at the weeds ; we may down with 'em,
but look out, for they're always ready to come
up again, and it'll be so to the end of the
chapter. If any of you think you are men
enough to do this of yourselves, you're
mightily mistaken. But you're promised
help; and you'll find it in a book more
worth reading than any other, tho' it may
lay on your shelves and be never looked at,
and, if your house is untidy, be covered with
dust. Now what I want us all to do is, to
read this book just as we read the gardening
ones, and, while we work away in our gardens, abide by its "calendar of operations" for
working at the heart. It's a shame such a
book should be so neglected.

Don't read it alone ; first get a good wife,
if you haven't one, and while she is at work
read to her and your children, if you have
any. Don't make a task-book of it, and,
take my word for it, there'll be something
wrong in yourselves if you don't find in it
comfort in sorrow, support in honest poverty,
something to keep you humble if you are
prosperous, and free from pride if you are
successful ; something to make you careful

how you speak of the faults of others, because you'll know so much of your own. It
will teach you to lend others a helping hand,
and to take help gratefully, if you ever need
it. It'll make you respectful to your employers, and will get you respect from them ;
and when you've roughed it through life,—
and I've known what it is to rough it as well
as any of you,—it will give you a hope
that'll grow stronger and stronger the older
you grow.

Good bye; I heartily wish you all well,
and that you'll make a deal better man
every way than your true friend,

JAMES GREGORY.

LONDON :
PRINTED BY LEVEY, ROBSON, AND FRANKLYN,
Great New Street and Fetter Lane.

.

www.ingramcontent.com/pod-product-compliance
Lightning Source LLC
Chambersburg PA
CBHW030608270326
41927CB00007B/1091

9783337129149